BELIEVE IN MIRACLES

Text copyright © Carmel Thomason 2016
The author asserts the moral right to be identified as the author of this work

Published by
The Bible Reading Fellowship
15 The Chambers, Vineyard
Abingdon, OX14 3FE
United Kingdom
Tel: +44 (0)1865 319700
Email: enquiries@brf.org.uk
Website: www.brf.org.uk
BRF is a Registered Charity

ISBN 978 0 85746 420 0
First published 2016
10 9 8 7 6 5 4 3 2 1 0
All rights reserved

Acknowledgements
Unless otherwise stated, scripture quotations are taken from The Holy Bible,
New International Version (Anglicised edition) copyright © 1979, 1984, 2011
by Biblica. Used by permission of Hodder & Stoughton Publishers, an Hachette
UK company. All rights reserved. 'NIV' is a registered trademark of Biblica.
UK trademark number 1448790.

Cover image: DAJ / Thinkstock.com

Every effort has been made to trace and contact copyright owners for material
used in this resource. We apologise for any inadvertent omissions or errors, and
would ask those concerned to contact us so that full acknowledgement can be
made in the future.

A catalogue record for this book is available from the British Library

Printed and bound by CPI Group (UK) Ltd, Croydon CR0 4YY

BELIEVE IN MIRACLES

A SPIRITUAL JOURNEY OF POSITIVE CHANGE

CARMEL THOMASON

For my parents, Harry and Eileen Thomason,
with appreciation and love

ACKNOWLEDGEMENTS

In many ways, for me, this book has been a journey of appreciation at the deepest level. The more I think about everything I have to be thankful for, the more I realise that I will only ever scrape the surface of recognising the good in my life for which I could give thanks. I will never know all the people who influence and shape my life in some way, but I am learning to say thank you more often and to feel that appreciation turn to love in my heart.

I would like to say a special thankyou to the following people who have helped me during the writing of this book. Thank you to Louise Houlder and Julie Corrigan, who listened to my idea as it was developing and were generous and encouraging in sharing views and experience. Thank you to Virginia Hearn, Aude Pasquier, Penny Glover and Sue Usher, who are always great encouragers of my work. Thank you to my aunt Mary White for her constant support, advice and guidance on scripture.

Thank you to Naomi Starkey and Karen Laister for believing in me and commissioning this book, Kristina Petersen for her expert eye in editing, Mike Parsons for overseeing the final stages to publication, and to all the wonderful team at BRF who have made this possible.

Thank you to my brother Paul, sister-in-law Lisa and nephew Zachary for their unwavering love, and to my parents, for whom a million thankyous will never feel enough.

CONTENTS

WEEK 4 REACH OUT

WEEK 5 LOVE YOUR LIFE

WEEK 6 BELIEVE IN MIRACLES

A NEW DAY

Jesus replied, 'Love the Lord your God with all your heart, with all your soul, and with all your mind.' This is the first and greatest commandment. The second is like it: 'Love your neighbour as you love yourself.' All the Law and the Prophets hang on these two commandments.

MATTHEW 22:37–40

Each morning we are given the miracle of a new day, so why do so many of us wake with feelings of dread or wanting to pull the covers back over our head? We all experience times when our lives don't feel like our own; when so many people and priorities want a piece of us that we don't know where to turn first. For many people, this overwhelming busyness has become the natural order of life. So often we wait until crises hit before we start re-evaluating our lives to make positive changes. It is at times like these, when it seems that there is nowhere left to turn, that we need to strip everything back and trust God to work change in our lives.

What if we didn't wait? What if we took a step back from the hustle and bustle of daily living to think about what we truly want from life? What if we decided to ask for God's help right now?

If you've picked up this book I'm guessing that you've got a heart for God, but sometimes life can get in the way of our best intentions. Jesus called us to love God and to love our neighbour. Two requests—that's it. So what happened to make our lives and our faith so complicated? We want to experience love, wonder, beauty, joy, and creativity, yet our reality is often something very different. We would like to feel more connected to ourselves, to God and to other people, but often we can't see how this could be possible.

In the next 40 days you will discover small practical steps you can take right now to help you make lasting changes towards a more prayerful, contented and connected life— improving your attitude towards yourself, deepening your relationship with God, and strengthening your relationships with others. You will also learn how to simplify your life to be more aligned with God's unique purpose for you, so that instead of being elusive, the enriching experiences of love, wonder, beauty, joy and creativity become part of your everyday.

I would encourage you to read no more than one day at a time. Some of the exercises involve activities as you go about your day, and it may be helpful to read a day ahead, so that you are ready to start when you wake. You may also find it useful to keep a journal of your thoughts as you go through each week, to help you recognise where God is working in your life and to be more open to his call.

None of us in life escapes suffering and on several occasions I have found myself stripping everything away and asking God, 'Where do I go from here?' It is a vulnerable position, but it can also be a very freeing one. This book has grown out of that prayer. We learn to lean on God by doing just that. Wherever you are in your spiritual journey right now, it's OK. God meets us where we are; all he asks is that we show up for our part. The miracle of the day is already yours; the adventure begins when you're open to experience it fully.

WEEK 1
BE STILL

Be still, and know that I am God.

PSALM 46:10

DAY 1

SILENCE

'Come with me by yourselves to a quiet place and get some rest.'
MARK 6:31

When I was a child, if my brother and I were squabbling in the car about what music to listen to, my mum would always chip in asking, 'When do I get what I want to listen to?'

'You never want to listen to anything,' we'd say in unison.

'That's right. I just want a bit of peace and quiet for a while. It's a choice to play nothing as well.'

'Well, when someone makes a record of silence, mum, you can have that,' I'd joke, but really I was annoyed. How was nothing a choice? A choice to be silent—at the time I couldn't think of anything more ridiculous or boring. Now that I am nearer the age my mum was then, I can understand better what she meant.

In today's 24-hour economy it has become increasingly difficult to find silent spaces, and for many people silence is so unusual that when they do experience it the feeling is uncomfortable rather than calming. From this perspective all silences are awkward ones, simply a void that needs to be filled quickly with something— chatter, music, television, computer games, internet surfing, whatever it may be.

For a long time it has been known that exposure to environmental noise, such as the sound of pneumatic drills, low-flying aircraft, road noise, loud music at 3 am or someone else's dog barking, adversely affects our health. Scientific studies have shown that being exposed to increased levels of environmental noise is linked to high blood pressure, heart disease, sleep disturbance and poor work performance.[1] The World Health Organisation has made recommendations for governments to introduce policies controlling environmental noise, but while other forms of environmental stress, such as second-hand smoke, dioxins and benzene, are falling, environmental noise is a problem that continues to increase. On an individual level there may be nothing we can do about this growing level of noise in our lives. Yet, what about the type of noise that can't be measured in scientific studies, the noise that we can do something about, the noise that we choose to experience every day? How much time do you spend watching TV, listening to the radio, playing music, surfing the internet or playing games using computers, tablets, or smartphones?

A report from the UK's TV Licensing revealed that we often underestimate just how much time we spend in these pursuits.[2] The majority of adults surveyed for the report claimed to watch less than 20 hours of TV a week, the equivalent of about three hours a day. However, official figures showed the true average to be more like 30 hours a week, or more than four hours a day. That's a lot of time, and doesn't include the time we spend watching video content on devices other than our TVs.

In highlighting this, I'm not suggesting that we stop watching our favourite TV shows, listening to music or connecting with friends online, but rather that we recognise the time we spend doing these things is a choice. I think these activities sometimes become such a part of our everyday life that we don't see them as an active choice, and we certainly don't realise the stress our need for constant entertainment might be causing. I know I didn't.

For a long time I was one of those people who filled every waking hour with noise of some sort. I'd wake up to the radio and fall asleep to music. I worked in a thriving city centre where the growth of new developments was fuelling a boom in the construction industry. Mine was an open plan office, a buzzing newsroom that was alive with conversation, ringing phones, and 24-hour news on the TV. It was lively and exciting! There was always something happening, and I never knew from one moment to the next what that might be.

I didn't understand why anyone would choose to spend time in silence. To me, silence was the same as doing nothing, and I always had to be doing something. Looking back, it's not surprising that I sometimes questioned the relevance of faith to my life. How could I hear from God if I never took the time to listen? God was always there; it was just that I was never still long enough to recognise him working in my life, or to hear the Spirit that he's placed in me, as he has in all of us.

All relationships need time devoted to them if they are to deepen, and our relationship with God is no different in that sense. You may have built some quiet time into your day already, but if you haven't, I'd encourage you, for each one of the 40 days of this journey, to spend some time in silence. If you are not used to this, it may feel like a challenge, and one I understand. It was difficult for me to do this at first, and I would often make excuses as to why I didn't have the time. There was always something more important to do. After all, doing something has got to trump doing nothing, hasn't it?

A wake-up call of any sort can be an excellent source of change, and for me it was clear that I was reaching burnout and needed to slow down. There was a church near where I worked at the time, called St Mary's, The Hidden Gem. If you are visiting Manchester, I would encourage you to stop by. The church is tucked away on Mulberry Street, between Deansgate and Albert Square. Inside you will find the 14 Stations of the Cross painted by the late Norman Adams in the early 1990s. Adams considered the paintings to be the greatest works of his life and there is no doubt that they attract a lot of people into the building. However, the peacefulness of the space, to be found just off one of the city's main shopping streets, will no doubt stay in the mind equally as much. The church was originally built in 1794 in an attempt to address the need of those living in poor-quality housing in what was then one of the city's most deprived and troubled areas. Writing in his *History of the Diocese of Manchester* the Reverend Arthur J. Dobb, comments, 'St Mary's much rebuilt, still stands on the same plot of land, now surrounded by the edifices of sophisticated materialism, which is probably more spiritually barren ground than the moral vileness of the 18th century.'[3]

I'm not sure that the city of Manchester is any more spiritually barren than any other major urban area, but I am pleased that the church is there and that its doors are open during the day to anyone who wants to escape the hustle and bustle of daily life, if just for a moment, to reconnect with their higher purpose and to find some peace.

It was only after I had been visiting the church regularly for several weeks that I began to notice that I missed that quiet time on days when I didn't go. I began to think about this time spent in silence, as the Bible describes it, as spending time in the presence of God. Indeed, even Jesus needed that, and would go off to quiet places, to be alone and pray (Luke 5:16). Why had I believed that I could be different, that I could feel close to God without spending any quality time with him?

I have been spending quiet time with God each day for more than ten years now, and in that time I have come to view these moments as a privilege rather than a chore. Before I began spending quiet time with God, I hadn't realised just how noisy my own thoughts were. Most mornings when I woke up, my mind would feel like a busy train station because there were so many different thoughts rushing through it. I used to think that was normal, because it was for me. After a couple of months of spending regular quiet time with God, I began to wake up feeling more refreshed and calmer. My runaway brain, which I'd thought was so much a part of myself, didn't need to be that way. It was a gradual change and one that I only really noticed when a stressful situation would arise and I'd realise that I wasn't reacting as strongly as I might once have done. Things that at one time would have upset me, I began to brush aside or bounce back from much more easily.

To give you a simple example, I was recently travelling on a train that was delayed. The journey should have taken almost three hours, so an extra 40 minutes meant that I was beginning to feel tired and hungry, and there was no restaurant car on board. Once off the train I was told that the tram service to my home was not running and I had to wait 20 minutes for a replacement bus. Unfortunately, the bus didn't drive me the whole way home; instead it stopped for me to pick up a tram which was running several stops down the road. Another problem was that the bus couldn't pull up alongside this tram stop. So, I had to cross a busy dual carriageway in the dark and walk for three minutes, pulling a heavy case behind me, to get to the tram stop, which was raised on a high platform, and the escalator wasn't working so I had to haul my luggage up two flights of steps, where I waited in the cold for another ten minutes until a tram arrived to take me home. What should have been a 15 minute journey from the station ended up taking me more than an hour.

The reason I'm telling you this in wearisome detail is to explain that it wasn't that I didn't notice all the delays or inconveniences of my journey. I did notice them, but I also realised that they didn't bother me in a way that they might have done years ago. At one time I would have been irritated by each minor mishap, and I would probably have moaned to anyone who would listen about the unreliability of public transport. This time that familiar churning of anxiety wasn't there; instead, I opened my front door feeling pleased to be home and was able to enjoy the rest of my evening.

Of course, I still sometimes get caught up in the busyness of life, as we all can, and rush ahead with my day without taking some time out simply to be. However, I notice that when I take the time to make silence with God a regular part of my day, small daily irritations don't seem to have such an impact on me. The feeling of inner calm that comes from taking time to nourish my spirit is not simply a feeling; it is a strength which allows me to view my life with greater perspective; to listen to the still small voice inside me; to notice where God is working in my life; to save my energy for where my actions can make a positive difference, and, as my family has noticed, to be a better person to be around.

There are many ways you can build quiet time into your

day, and how you do it is up to you. I find it best to get up 15 minutes earlier and make space first thing in the morning. That way I know that there is no chance that the time I've set aside for silence will be squeezed out by other activities of the day.

Before you begin, find a place where you won't be disturbed. If this is difficult, explain to your family what you are doing so that they can support you. If all else fails, find somewhere quiet outside your home—drive to work 15 minutes early and park up in your car, find a nearby church, or lock yourself in the bathroom if it's the only place you know you'll not be disturbed.

Find a comfortable position, preferably sitting upright; close your eyes, and take a couple of good deep breaths to help relax your body, before allowing your breath to return to normal. Imagine you are breathing in God's love and breathing out anything that is troubling you.

If you are new to any form of meditation or contemplative prayer, you may find that quietening the mind is not always as simple as relaxing the body. Don't worry, you are far from alone in this! According to scientists at the University of California and Los Angeles Laboratory of Neuro Imaging, the average person has 70,000 thoughts a day. That's the equivalent of almost 50 thoughts a minute or one every second. In sitting quietly, it's important to recognise that we are not attempting to empty our mind of thoughts, but we can quieten them down, so that instead of being caught up in mental patterns that tie us to the past or propel us to the future, we experience life more presently and in doing so experience God at the heart of our being.

Repetitive phrases or mantras can help to quieten the mind. You may want to use a verse of scripture, or a simple phrase such as, 'I am filled with the healing love of God'. The World Community for Christian Meditation (WCCM) based on the teaching of Benedictine monk, John Main, suggests using the Aramaic word, *maranatha*, which means, 'Come, Lord Jesus.' It is the word that Paul uses to end his first letter to the Corinthians (1 Corinthians 16:22) and John uses it at the close of the book of Revelation (Revelation 22:20). You can use the English translation if you like, although many people find the Aramaic form helpful because for most people it doesn't have any images associated with it. Experiment with a few words or phrases until you find a form of words that works for you.

Repeat your chosen phrase slowly in your mind. Don't worry if your thoughts wander to something else—this is normal. When you notice this happening, don't follow your thought. By that, I mean that if you think about what you are going to cook for dinner, don't start considering options or preparing a meal in your mind; simply bring your thoughts back to your chosen phrase. Do this each time your thoughts wander, and you will find that in time your mind settles down. If you find that you can't relax because you are concerned about the time, particularly if you are finding space for God before leaving for work, you can set a timer. There are many timers and stopwatches available, but I like to use the WCCM timer that can be downloaded for free as part of the WCCM app.

If you are not used to taking time out to be with God in silence, it may feel at first as if nothing is happening and you may have the urge to get up and do other things. Don't worry about this. In time you will find that this silent space and closeness to God that you are cultivating will start to stay with you as a deeper sense of calm as you go through the rest of your day. You may not even notice it yourself until someone else points it out to you. As my brother said to me, 'What's happened to you? When did you get so patient?' How do I begin to answer that? I didn't need to do anything. I simply opened my heart to God, and he did the rest.

TODAY'S PRACTICE

1 Find 15 minutes in your day to sit quietly, close your eyes, take in a couple of deep breaths to help you relax, and be still in the presence of God. Imagine you are breathing in God's love and breathing out anything that is troubling you.

2 Chose a word or phrase that is comforting for you and repeat it gently in your mind. Examples you might want to try are: '*maranatha*'; 'I am filled with the healing love of God'; 'I can do all things through Christ who strengthens me'. If your thoughts wander, don't worry about this; it is normal. When this happens, simply notice it and bring your thoughts back to your chosen word or phrase.

3 We are going to be doing this practice every day for the next 40 days, so in that time you can experiment to see what is the best way within your lifestyle to fit in some silent time each day. There is no right or wrong way to make time to listen to God; the important thing is to find a way that works for you.

REMEMBER THE GOOD

If anything is excellent or praiseworthy—think about such things.

PHILIPPIANS 4:8

Do you ever have one of those days when nothing seems to go right? First the alarm fails to go off and, realising you've slept in, you stub your toe while getting out of bed too quickly. Brushing your teeth in haste, you end up splashing toothpaste on your shirt, and you have to leave the house with a wet patch where you'd tried to wash it off because you didn't have time to iron anything else to wear. When you finally get on your way after ten minutes, you find your car sitting bumper-to-bumper on the road, random horns keep beeping, and, although the traffic lights seem to be changing, nothing is moving because other people, who are probably also rushing like you, have thought it a good idea to enter the box junction and block the traffic from moving in any direction. Oh, did I forget to mention, it's raining and you've forgotten your umbrella, so the walk from the car park to the office isn't going to be much fun. Unfortunately, it doesn't get any better once you get to work, because there are lots of changes going on and most people feel over-worked, disgruntled and insecure. At lunchtime your daughter rings you. She's in tears about something that's happened at school and, as much as you try to, you don't understand what she's talking about; then you get home to find the cat has vomited on the duvet, and your friend has left a message on voicemail cancelling the one evening you were looking forward to all week.

On days like these it's tempting to think that life stinks. OK, nothing that people might consider 'really bad' has happened, but you're just worn down under the weight of a thousand little miseries and it feels as if there's no enjoyment in life any more. We've all had such days, perhaps not with the same experiences, but filled with minor calamities and irritations. When we feel like this it's easy for the bad to overcrowd the good, sometimes to the extent that we think everything is wrong and nothing is right.

There have been occasions in my life when 'wrong side of the bed' days became my norm. These have nearly always been during times of prolonged stress. Perhaps, like me at those times, you have good reason to feel as if life has handed you a raw deal. Perhaps you've lost a loved one; your relationship has broken down; your job has been made redundant; or you've got a bad prognosis for your health. We can't ignore these things and pretend that they are not happening, but if we are truly to believe what Paul said in his letter to the Romans, that all things work together for good (Romans 8:28), we need to stay open to recognising the good when God places it on our path.

Easier said than done, you might say. I know. I might not have experienced exactly the same circumstances as the ones you are facing right now, but I have been through times when I could find no rest in sleep and yet when morning came I found it a struggle to lift my head from the pillow because I couldn't face what the day might bring.

At times like these I've taken comfort in the words Paul wrote in his first letter to the Corinthians in which he explains that the temptations and trials we face in life are experienced by many other people (1 Corinthians 10:13). Reading this passage reminds me that, however I might be feeling in the moment, I am not alone. God never promises that life will be easy, but when we are struggling he promises to be alongside us, offering a loving refuge in which we can rest and gain strength (Psalm 46:1).

It was at one such time, several years ago now, that I began keeping a note of good things that happened to me during the day. To try to do as Paul preached, and to fill my mind with things that are good and deserve praise: things that are true, noble, right, pure, lovely and admirable (Philippians 4:8). I bought a 'week to view' diary just for this purpose, and each evening before I went to bed I wrote down everything good that had happened in the day. The rules were that I had to make sure I filled the space for that day's diary entry; I could write only good things, and whatever I wrote had to have happened that day. If Paul could speak with such confidence and joy while imprisoned by the Romans, then the least I could do was to recognise some of his wisdom and try to apply it to my own life.

At first, I found it difficult to think of anything good that was happening because my mind was so preoccupied with my troubles. That was precisely why I had decided to keep a list of good things God was doing for me, because I knew that there must be some good in my life somewhere—I just couldn't see it. It wasn't that I wanted to deny the difficult stuff happening. I was all too aware of that side of my life, but I needed another perspective, something to help me deal with my problems, or to let them pass, or whatever I needed to do to feel that life was worth living again. What I didn't need to do, and what I was in danger of doing, was to turn whatever was happening now into the story of the rest of my life.

We've all done it—turned our current situation into a negative vision for our future, thinking, I'll never get well, I'll never find a job, I'll never get out of debt, I'll never kick this addiction, I'll never find the right relationship, I'll never make friends, I'll never be able to afford my own home, I'll never lose weight... the list goes on. We take our situation as it is now and we can't see how life can ever improve. I'd done that so many times and I was trying not to do it again.

The previous year while I was travelling in Europe I met a young woman who had been divorced for a couple of years. She talked at great length about her ex-husband, going over and over what had happened during their marriage, to try to understand where things had started to go wrong. As much as she talked, she never did come up with any answers, none that she could be certain of anyway. She even began to question if her whole marriage had been a lie—if her ex-husband had ever loved her at all. I understood that she needed to talk, but I also noticed how she moved from talking about her ex-husband to making sweeping statements about the rest of her life. 'I'll never find anyone to love me,' she said and I could tell from her tone and expression that when she spoke those words, she truly believed them.

Looking from the outside, that vision of her future seemed so unlikely. Until she had opened her heart to me that wasn't how I saw her at all. I saw her as an attractive, well dressed, independent woman who was friendly and outgoing. Why would I have struck up a conversation with her if she was such an unlovable person, as she perceived herself to be? From listening to her talk, you'd think that there was nothing good in her life, but I only had to look at her and our surroundings to see that wasn't true. If I'm truly honest, I also sympathised because I recognised myself in some of the things she said. I'd thought similar things about myself in the past and had believed them too. When we hear our own words come back to us from someone else, we can realise just how self-pitying we must sound, and self-pity is never an attractive emotion. There were plenty of good things to thank God for in her life, even if it was simply the sunshine, the fresh food and the sea view we enjoyed that afternoon.

Sometimes it can be hard to notice the good things that are right in front of us for all to see. When I first started writing down good things that had happened each day, I struggled to fill that small space with anything. I started giving myself little treats so that I would have something good to write down. I did things like putting fresh sheets on my bed so that I could write: I have clean sheets and my bed feels cosy and warm. I'd buy a glass of fresh orange juice at lunchtime and savour the taste of it, or go for a walk after work and watch the sunset.

Once I started looking for items to write down, I began noticing a lot more good things happening. Someone would hold a door open for me while I was out shopping, a driver would wave me through the traffic, or a friend would give me a compliment. Each time something nice happened in my day I'd think, great, I need to remember that, it's something to add to my list. I think a lot of these small kindnesses were probably happening all the time, but I had stopped noticing them.

After a while I didn't need to try to fill the space with good things, because on most days I could have filled the space many times over. I could see the good in life again because I was looking for it, and it was only a couple of months before my circumstances began to improve in ways that I could never have imagined.

Since then, I haven't always kept my 'good news diary' every day, but I've found that when I do, it helps me to keep a better perspective on life. Like everyone I still go through trying times, and I've found that those are the times when I get the most benefit from this daily practice. These days I use a small notebook and use a page for each day, and on any days when, for whatever reason, I don't write in the book, I always make a mental list in my head on going to bed and give thanks to God for everything on it.

Sometimes I re-read what I've written months later and it helps me to see my life in greater perspective. I know when I was going through a particularly difficult time, but I also see pages of small kindnesses and blessings, which I could have so easily overlooked. They shine through like rays of hope, a reminder that however dark our circumstances are, the darkness is never the whole story.

TODAY'S PRACTICE

1 Find 15 minutes in your day to sit quietly, close your eyes, take in a couple of deep breaths to help you relax, and be still in the presence of God. Imagine you are breathing in God's love and breathing out anything that is troubling you.

2 Get yourself a pocket notebook or a 'week to view' pocket diary that you will use only for the purpose of this exercise.

3 At the end of the day, spend five minutes thinking about any good things that have happened and things that you have enjoyed. The task is to fill the space for the day's diary entry. Don't stop writing until the space is full. It doesn't matter how

big or small the thing is that you choose to write down. All that matters is that you are noting something to thank God for and that it happened today. If you have to give yourself a treat so that you have something good to write down, then do it.

DAY 3

PRAY ABOUT EVERYTHING

Do not be afraid; do not be discouraged, for the Lord your
God will be with you wherever you go.

JOSHUA 1:9

When I was younger I lived for a few years in a flat
overlooking a church. I had a wonderful view of the church
spire and gardens from my window, and for the most part it
was a very peaceful place to call home. Occasionally, though,
I'd hear what sounded like arguing outside and I'd look to see
a man standing at the edge of the church grounds shouting
at God about the troubles of his life. It was almost as if he'd
thought, 'I'm going to march down to that house of God and
tell him what for.'

Each time this happened, I wanted to open the window
and shout back, 'You can argue with God just as easily
from outside your own house as you can outside mine.' Of
course I didn't, because the poor man was clearly distressed
and it seemed best that he take his anger out on God, who
can more than handle anything we care to throw at him.
However, I found it interesting to think about how we can
take a common phrase about the church being the house of
God quite literally.

Now, I know not many of us will have expressed such a
display of emotion outside a church, but many people, and I
am one of them, have often confined God to certain spaces
or times in life. We may think about God when we are in

church or when we are praying in the morning and evening, but outside of those times, we never think to ask for God's help, and often go through the day as if we were alone and having to work out every problem we face in our own strength. In doing so, our idea of God as being somewhere else isn't as obvious as the man shouting outside God's house hoping to be heard, but aren't we putting God in a box just the same?

It's good to take time out to spend quietly with God in prayer, but in doing that we also need to be careful that we're not keeping him in our little 'prayer box', and making prayer an event rather than a way of life as Paul talks about it when he urges us to pray always, for all people and on every occasion as the Spirit leads (Ephesians 6:18). Prayer doesn't needs to be complicated, or restricted to a particular time, place or form of words. It's not something that we need to do, but something that we are privileged to be able to do. We have free access to God wherever and whenever we want, completely unrestricted. When I really stop to think about what that means for me, the idea is almost too wonderful to grasp. It makes me wonder whether we keep God in a box because we take his 24-hour-seven-day-a-week access for granted, or is it the idea that God is really there for us all the time so generous and amazing that we don't allow ourselves truly to believe it?

I've heard it said many times that there are no atheists in the emergency room. Well, I don't know if there are or there aren't, but I do know that when times get tough I've often reached out to God in prayer as a last resort rather than as a first response. So often, I try to work everything out for myself, to push and push when situations don't appear to be going the way I would like them to. Only when all else fails do I turn to God and ask for help. If I really believed that God was beside me always, and that his Spirit lives in me, wouldn't I ask for his help and advice in everything I did? Wouldn't I at least speak to him more often and listen to what he might have to say?

I wondered what it would feel like to live as if I believed fully in my heart that God is with me wherever I go. What confidence would I feel from knowing that whatever situation I face, I never need to face it alone because God is there, always alongside me?

I began to realise that, however I might have felt, God was never distant from me. Rather, I was distancing myself from God, and in doing so I was failing to recognise the love and support that was there for me all along. I was the one who had to change and become more open to God, but how could I do it, especially when I felt so downhearted? In my quiet time with God, I started to ask God to help me to accept his love and to keep me near him. Whenever I felt anxious about a situation, I began repeating in my mind the words God spoke to Joshua and reminding myself of Jesus' words following his resurrection, 'I am with you always, to the very end of the age' (Matthew 28:20). After doing this for a while, I noticed that I felt far less anxious in all kinds of situations. I'd do something and only later think, 'At one time that situation would have made me very anxious.' Indeed, sometimes it was difficult for me to remember what it was that I had been so anxious about in the first place.

Once I began to think of prayer as simply a conversation with God, I found myself talking to him as I went through my day, the same as I would if he were a friend beside me. I began to pray about everything and for anyone who came to mind who might be in need in any way. For example, if

I was going into an important meeting at work, I'd thank God for being with me, for always supporting me, and I'd ask him to help me perform my best for myself and for everyone involved. If I was stuck in traffic because of an accident or I heard an emergency siren, I'd say a little prayer, 'God, please look after that person in trouble and keep them close to you.' If I heard about some trouble on the news, I'd pray for the person affected there and then. If someone told me about a difficult situation in their life, I would silently pray for them and ask God to show me if there was any way I could be of help.

There are some situations in which we can do something practical to help, but there are others in which there is nothing practical we can do. In praying about these situations almost as soon as I heard about them, I started to feel less helpless and it also made the situation feel less hopeless. If we ask God to place on our hearts anything that we can do, we can play our part and rest assured that he will take care of the rest. For, however hopeless a situation looks, God will do as he did for Joseph when his brothers sold him into slavery, and take what was meant for harm and use it for good in the lives of many people (Genesis 50:20).

Today, our practice is to be more open to God, to his plan for our life and for what he might ask us to do as our part in that. Whatever you are feeling, let him know. If you're angry, tell him—God can cope with your anger. If you're fearful, tell him and ask him to give you strength. If you are enjoying something, share your joy by saying thank you. If you want to pray for someone, then pray for them. You don't need to ask permission to pray for someone, and you don't need to do it out loud so everyone can hear, or even to let that person know that you hold them in your prayers. If you don't know what to do in a certain situation, ask God to put the best action for all concerned on your heart. Sometimes there won't be anything we can do, and we can be OK with that too, because we know that God has it in his hands and will work all things out for good.

In recognising God's presence in everything I do, I have become not only more connected to God, but also more connected to my deepest needs, and my connection to others has been strengthened too. For me that is the real power of prayer. It keeps us all connected, as one, to each other and to God, our creator.

I hope that today, through this exercise, you will begin to experience fully in your heart the truth that God is with you wherever you go, right here, right now and always, until the end of time.

TODAY'S PRACTICE

1 Find 15 minutes in your day to sit quietly, close your eyes, take in a couple of deep breaths to help you relax, and be still in the presence of God. Imagine you are breathing in God's love and breathing out anything that is troubling you.

2 As you go through your day, talk to God regularly, as you would to a friend beside you. Pray about everything and for anyone who comes to mind who might be in need in any way. Stay open to God, so that you become more aware of where he may be working in your life and what he might be asking of you.

3 At the end of the day, spend five minutes thinking about any good things that have happened and things that you have enjoyed. Fill the space for today's diary entry. Don't stop

writing until the space is full. It doesn't matter how big or small the thing is that you choose to write down. All that matters is that you are noting something good that happened today. When you have written your list, thank God for all the things that are on it.

DAY 4

ENJOY THE MOMENT

Why, you do not even know what will happen tomorrow.
What is your life? You are a mist that appears for a little while
and then vanishes.
JAMES 4:14

How many times have you said, 'I'll be happy when…' or 'I'll do that when I finish my degree, when I get a new job, when I get married, when I have a family of my own, when the children have left school, when I pay off my mortgage, when I retire… when…' It's as if we're putting a hold on enjoying life until sometime in the future when all our troubles will be sorted out and everything will be OK.

There are other times in our life when we get caught in the habit of always looking back, wishing things were how they used to be and talking about the good old days.

Then there are times when we are not so obviously living in the future or the past, but the here and now is passing us by just the same—times when we are simply caught up in a haze of being busy, rushing from one place to another, from one activity to another, without ever pausing to enjoy any of it. In all these situations life can feel like a treadmill with no 'off' switch. We're running just to stand still. However fast we run, it's never fast enough and we never seem to get to where we want to be.

However quickly we can do something, we or someone else will want it to be done quicker. I see people getting visibly stressed on the London Underground because they have narrowly missed a tube, even though there will be another one along in two minutes. I laugh about that, but then in Manchester, where I live, I find myself getting irritated if I miss a tram when there is another coming along in six minutes. Instead of feeling grateful that I have such a fantastic transport network in the city (when some areas of the country only have one bus a week, and many parts of the world don't even have roads), I find it a cause of frustration.

It is the same on the roads. There are increasing incidents of road rage because people feel they aren't getting where they want to be fast enough. There are even incidents of trolley rage in supermarkets, because customers cannot get their trolley down the grocery aisle at an agreeable speed. The faster life gets, the faster we want and expect it to be, but even if someone invented teleporting, would we be satisfied? The attitude that leads us to think that we'll be happy when we reach a certain goal is the same one that will move the goal posts for our happiness when we get there. If we are always looking to the past or the future, or we are forever caught up in a general busyness, how will we recognise when God places something special on our path? We may complain that our prayers are not heard, yet how can we be sure of that when our eyes and ears are closed to the answers?

I was once a regular at a café where two men, who worked nearby, would often call in for lunch. They never spoke to me or to anyone else in the small café, but sometimes they would sit on an adjacent table and, unintentionally, I would catch parts of their conversation. Aside from what was going on at work, the main topic they talked about was the younger man's love life, or lack of love life. Well, it wasn't so much a conversation as a one-way train of thought—

the younger man talked at great length while the older man ate his sandwich and nodded occasionally in the right places. The younger man had begun dating on the internet, which in itself seemed a good idea as he was keen to meet someone special, although it wasn't working out the way he had planned. He complained about several women with whom he'd had an online correspondence, speculating and building up all kinds of possible scenarios about relationships with women he had yet to meet. This situation went on for months and each time the men came in, the younger always appeared unhappy. I looked around the café and there were lots of young women eating alone every day, yet the man never thought to look up from his lunch to smile, or to try to strike up a conversation. God was probably placing suitable women on his path all the time, but he was too busy complaining about how things weren't working out for him in the world of internet dating even to notice them.

I thought about that man and wondered if there were any areas in my life where I was being equally blinded. Were there things in my life that were not going as planned, but because I was so focused on doing something one particular way, I couldn't see other possibilities God was opening up to me?

I remember taking my puppy for one of his first walks. We were only a couple of steps from my house when he stopped and began sniffing the air. I looked up to see a tree full of scented spring blossom. The flowers were a blush of pink above me, yet were it not for my dog, Sam, I could so easily have walked by without noticing the beauty right in front of me. It's like that old saying about taking time to stop and smell the roses; except that I didn't need to take time out to enjoy the flowers—they were right there in front of me.

The reason I hadn't seen them was because my mind was somewhere else, running ahead, already planning where I was going and what I'd be doing later.

It is good to make plans, but it is also easy to over-complicate our lives by mistaking always looking ahead and living in the future for being organised. An example of this is thinking about what you are going to cook for dinner while you're eating breakfast. It's hard truly to enjoy one meal when you're thinking about another one. I see this happening in so many people's lives—their minds are rushing ahead to the next thing before they've enjoyed what they are doing right now, or they are sitting in front of someone and their eyes are blank because their thoughts are elsewhere.

There is nothing worse that talking to someone who is constantly looking over your shoulder or checking a mobile phone. The most charismatic people in life are those who make the other person feel as if they are, at least for that moment, the most important person in the world. Some American presidents and Hollywood film stars are forever being praised for this quality. It is a wonderful attribute, but it is one that we can all have, and it is one the Bible encourages us to develop. It comes from being present in the moment and giving your full attention to what God is doing right here and right now. Our minds may be full, thinking about all kinds of issues, but as Jesus says, we cannot add any time to our life by worrying about it. He gives us the strength to handle what we are doing now, and he will give us the strength to face tomorrow's worries when that time comes (Matthew 5:34). So often we find ourselves struggling because we want the strength right now to work out all our problems from yesterday, today, and ten years down the line. Is it any wonder that we get overwhelmed?

At one time, I used to be that person—the one who looked like she was carrying the troubles of the world on her shoulders. I was what you might call a natural-born worrier and lived in my head more than in the world. If we're not careful, we can develop the habit of thinking about being somewhere else, doing something else, with someone else. It wasn't intentional, but there were times in my life when wonderful things were happening that I failed to appreciate. I didn't experience all the joy that was open to me because I was too busy worrying about what might or might not happen and often didn't. I've now learned through experience to live one day at a time and to replace worrying thoughts when they come up (and they often still do) with a focus on what God is doing in my life right now. Paul says that if we place our trust in God, his power within us will help us to accomplish far and beyond anything we could even dream about (Ephesians 3:17–21). That has certainly been true for me, and I'm sure it will be for you too.

Even if it's just for today, make an effort to live in the moment. Take time to listen to the people you are with; notice the environment you are in; take a couple of seconds to smell the blossom or watch the sunset; sit down to eat and savour the taste your food; smile at the server on the checkout counter; notice who is travelling with you on the train or sitting next to you in the canteen; wave to your neighbour; if you're at work then concentrate on the task in hand as it'll make the time go quicker if nothing else, and who knows you may find something in it you enjoy.

Don't let another minute of your life pass you by without really living it. Accept that God has placed you where you are for a reason and make an effort to be fully present wherever you are, whatever you are doing, and whoever you are with.

TODAY'S PRACTICE

1 Find 15 minutes in your day to sit quietly, close your eyes, take in a couple of deep breaths to help you relax, and be still in the presence of God. Imagine you are breathing in God's love and breathing out anything that is troubling you.

2 Whatever you are doing today try to be truly present while you are doing it. Notice where your thoughts are and if they are rushing ahead or pulling you back, try to bring them back to where you are now. If you are spending time with your children, then spend time with your children—don't be thinking about the report you've got to do for work. Accept that God has placed you wherever you are for a reason and, although you may not always understand it, be open to where he might be working in your life, do what you are doing with a good heart, and know that you are exactly where you are meant to be.

3 At the end of the day, spend five minutes thinking about any good things that have happened and things that you have enjoyed. Fill the space for today's diary entry. Don't stop writing until the space is full. It doesn't matter how big or small the thing is that you choose to write down. All that matters is that you are noting something good that happened today. When you have written your list, thank God for all the things that are on it.

SPEAK KINDLY

Gracious words are a honeycomb, sweet to the soul and
healing to the bones.

PROVERBS 16:24

I remember when I was a teenager my mum always used to
say to me, 'Carmel, if you've not got something nice to say
about somebody then it's best to say nothing at all.'

'But, mum,' I'd whine, 'you don't know what they did...
It's not fair... Why can't you just be on my side?'

It's funny, isn't it, how having someone agree with us
while we vent our emotions can make us feel as if we are
being supported; as if the person who is agreeing is on our
side. Of course, my mum wants the best for me and is always
on my side, as I put it then. That was probably precisely why
she didn't join in the complaining, and although I didn't
understand it at the time, her response was healthier for
me. Obviously she would listen to me, for hours on end
sometimes, if I was trying to work out a problem or talk
through a situation, but for me simply to be nasty about
someone who had been nasty to me, or to moan about how
bad things were or how awful someone was, was not going
to change my situation. By agreeing with me, my mum
would only have made me feel justified in being so upset or
vengeful. Going over and over the situation was only going
to keep it in my thoughts for longer, so that I became even
more hyped up about whatever was bothering me.

Yet, the fact that I wanted my mum to join in my complaint shows how easy it is for us to feel like we're bonding when we complain. In doing so we feel better for a short while, but research has shown that teenage girls who talk excessively about their problems are more likely to develop depression and anxiety, and the same is likely to be true for adults.[4]

I'd like to say that I learned this lesson fully while I was a teenager, but it didn't come easy to me to live as the Bible teaches and do all things without grumbling, fault-finding and complaining (Philippians 2:14). Something would go wrong in my day and I'd end up telling my friends and my boyfriend and my parents—anyone who would listen. I'd also get caught up in other people's grumblings. In my first job, talking about how bad things were would make me feel like 'part of the gang', but then I ended up getting so dissatisfied and frustrated that I had no option but to look for another job. After I'd left, a wise woman said to me that she thought it was unfair of some of the older workers to complain constantly about the workplace to me, because if it was so bad how come they were still there years later?

I often think about that, because even if we are in a situation that we can't change, complaining isn't going to make us feel any better, and most often it makes us feel worse.

I'm not saying that we shouldn't ever complain if things aren't right, but usually we're not complaining to the person who can do anything about it, nor are we looking for solutions we might have ourselves.

A few months back I was talking to one of my neighbours, who was being very downbeat. We live in a part of the city where there are a lot of outside visitors, and he was grumbling about the amount of litter on the street. He went on to say that that he was unhappy about living here for a lot of reasons, and after several minutes of complaining he even went so far as to say that he was sure he could find somewhere else to live that was better maintained. I didn't think that our street had a bigger problem with litter than any other major urban area has, but after our conversation I started to notice it more and I also noticed that I was becoming dissatisfied with my home. I've always loved living where I do, so when I recognised this feeling inside me, it wasn't something that I wanted.

Later that week I was speaking to another neighbour and mentioned it to her. 'Well, he's not alone there,' she told me. 'A lot of people are complaining about the amount of litter left by visitors.' 'The council need to clean up round here more often,' another neighbour complained, and yet another complained about the number of visitors and explained that's why we should have 'residents only' parking on the road.

Before long, everyone was grumbling and increasingly frustrated about the litter on our street and started to feel resentful about strangers, who were possibly making a mess and who were taking up parking spaces in our area. I wasn't exempt from this, and the constant complaining began to get me down, so that every time I saw an empty crisp packet or takeaway bag on the road I felt a twinge of irritation that fed my general dissatisfaction.

I didn't want to feel this way, so I began reminding myself of all the reasons why I enjoyed living where I do. We get lots of visitors because it is a lovely place. People want to come here for a day out, and we get to live here all the time—how cool is that? It also wasn't true that the council didn't clean the street. I saw street cleaners on a regular basis, but they can't be there to pick up each time someone decides to leave their empty takeaway packet by the side of the road, or to have a picnic and not take their rubbish with them when they leave.

I got together with another neighbour, who is a friend, and started talking about what we could do. We couldn't stop people visiting the area; we couldn't stop some people dropping litter and we couldn't get the council to do a daily litter patrol, but we could pick up the litter ourselves. Surely that would be better than walking past some litter, feeling annoyed, complaining about how disgusting some people are and how badly maintained the area is, and then feeling even more stressed when we walk past again to see the same litter still there. I said that I wouldn't mind doing a weekly or monthly litter pick with whoever wanted to join us. Perhaps it could even be a way of getting to know more of our neighbours.

So, that is what we did. Another neighbour called the council who agreed to provide us with litter picking equipment for several people, and what had once been a cause for dissatisfaction in the community became a way to bring us together. The problem was the same, but we were working towards a solution rather than constantly grumbling about it, and the result was uplifting.

That situation worked out well, but it could so easily have tipped the other way. I've seen it happen so often in many situations, particularly in relationships, when people begin to take each other for granted and focus on small things that irritate them, rather than on all the things they love about that person. There is nothing that will destroy a relationship faster than fault-finding, no matter what relationship it is. Someone can be 95 per cent amazing but if we focus on the five per cent we'd like to change, in the end that five per cent of the person's character that annoys us is all we can see. So many marriages fail this way, with people going their separate ways in search of that missing five per cent. When they find those qualities in someone new they are happy for a while, until they realise the new person isn't 100 per cent perfect either.

Mother Teresa (1910–97) said, 'Kind words can be short and easy to speak but their echoes are truly endless.' She was right. It is as easy to say something good as it is to say something bad, but it doesn't always feel that way, does it? Most of the time, when people say something unpleasant, they don't do so because they are consciously meaning to do harm; it's just a habit they've grown into. I used to work with a woman who would always tell me if someone had said something nasty about me and then repeat what was said. At the end of whatever she was telling me she'd always add, 'I always say forewarned is forearmed.' She was justifying telling me those things by saying she was helping me. Hearing those words didn't help me in any way. They just hurt me and made me suspicious of people with whom I might otherwise have had a good relationship. After all, hasn't each one of us said something about someone at some time to let off steam? So what if a person didn't like me? Did I need to know? I didn't need to be forearmed—I was going into work, not into battle. Everyone can't like everyone; even when there is a landslide election victory there is still usually more than half of the population who wanted someone else to win. Of course, I didn't think that at the time. Instead I found myself getting caught up in negative talk, which I thought was bringing us closer in friendship, but in reality wasn't doing either of us any good.

When I think about those times it reminds me of a friend

at university who ended her relationship because she said she'd noticed her boyfriend's feet stuck out to the side when he cycled and it made her feel sick. If you want to find fault with other people, there will always be something. The same is true for your career, your home, or anything else in the world. There is always plenty to grumble and complain about, but I've found that the opposite is also true.

Grumbling about the world used to be a habit for me. Now, I make a conscious effort to notice when I'm doing it. Of course, I still do, but when I notice myself falling into that way of talking, I think, 'Is there something I can do about this problem?' Or, if it's a person I'm talking about, I stop myself and think about all the reasons I love that person and everything I have to be grateful to them for. If it's someone I struggle to feel positive feelings about, I'll do as my mum advised all those years ago, and maybe get it off my chest once and then leave it at that. I don't need to relive a horrible conversation, or go on and on about something awful that has happened. I'm sure too that other people don't need or want to hear it.

I've also made an effort where I can to say something positive. I don't say something untrue that I don't think or feel. Before, I would often think something nice about someone and never say it. What good is that to them? It's like when I left one of my jobs and everyone suddenly said all these nice things about me. I never realised how valued I was until then. I want people in my life to know how valuable they are to me, and how much I appreciate them being a part of my life. In being freer with my compliments, I'm reminding myself just how much beauty there is in the world and how much I have to be grateful for, and in so doing I've discovered that pleasant words, when spoken genuinely and from the heart, really are good for our mind, body and soul.

TODAY'S PRACTICE

1 Find 15 minutes in your day to sit quietly, close your eyes, take in a couple of deep breaths to help you relax, and be still in the presence of God. Imagine you are breathing in God's love and breathing out anything that is troubling you.

2 See if you can go for a day without complaining, grumbling, making cruel or negative remarks, or gossiping. If you find that you do say something negative, notice what you're doing and try to change the topic of conversation to something else, to focus on solutions rather than problems. If you find you are critical or angry about something, notice what it is. Is there something you can do to change the situation? Anger is just an emotion; it's what we do with it that counts. Also, take the opportunity to speak kind words to someone. If you think something nice about someone, be free with your compliments and let them know.

3 At the end of the day, spend five minutes thinking about any good things that have happened and things that you have enjoyed. Fill the space for today's diary entry. Don't stop writing until the space is full. It doesn't matter how big or small the thing is that you choose to write down. All that matters is that you are noting something good that happened today. When you have written your list, thank God for all the things that are on it.

LIVE BEYOND COMPARE

With whom, then, will you compare God? To what image
will you liken him?

ISAIAH 40:18

Some years ago, while working as a section editor on a
newspaper, I asked a young reporter who was working for
me to interview an actor who was making a comeback after
some time out of the spotlight. It was well reported that he'd
suffered a period of depression in the past, and the reporter
had come across this information as part of his research
before making the call. 'So, I read you've had depression,'
the young reporter said breezily. 'You've got everything.
You're good-looking; you're rich; you're on TV; you've got
women throwing themselves at you. What have you got to
be depressed about?' There was a pause. I then heard, 'Hello?
Hello?' The reporter turned to me, 'We've been cut off. There
must have been a bad signal.'

It was clear that the actor had decided to end their
conversation abruptly. The young reporter had shown no
sensitivity in his questioning or any understanding of mental
illness. Yet, although he'd done it in a clumsy way, I realised
that this reporter had simply done what so many of us do
all the time, myself included: we look at selected parts of
another person's life and think, 'I wish I had what they have.'

We never truly know what is happening in someone else's
life and what challenges they face. It's easy to stand on the

outside, looking in with envy, but as the old saying goes, if we threw all our problems in a pile and saw everyone else's, we'd pick our own back up.

Rarely do we compare all aspects of our life. Instead, we look at someone else's wealth and think, 'I wish I had that', or we look at their job, their car, their house, their exotic holiday, their relationship, their good looks... whatever it may be that we think we'd rather have. Of course, there is nothing wrong with wanting to better ourselves in any aspect of our lives, but there is a world of difference between healthy ambition and resentment that can build in our hearts from comparing ourselves unfavourably with others.

The Bible warns us not to covet our neighbour's goods or relationships because doing so only makes us unhappy with what we've got (Exodus 20:17). We could be in the top one per cent of earners and it might still not be enough. Indeed, research has recently shown this to be the case, with some people in this elite income bracket believing that they are hard up. It sounds ridiculous to most of us, but when these people look at the world's super-rich, they realise that they cannot enjoy the same lifestyle and so in their minds, they are convinced that they are badly off.[5] When I first read that, I thought, 'How do people become so deluded? How can they not realise how fortunate they are?' Yet, none of us are immune to that trap. Once we start to compare ourselves with others in any way, there is always going to be someone who has more, and no matter what we have, it will never be enough.

Life will often not be fair in our eyes. Jesus tells us as much himself in the parable of the vineyard. In the story, each of the men agrees to work for one coin, but then some become disgruntled when they discover that all men were paid equally, regardless of how many hours they had worked. On hearing their complaints, the owner of the vineyard says, 'Don't I have the right to do what I want with my own money? Or are you envious because I am generous?' (Matthew 20:15).

Jesus ends the parable by saying, 'So the last will be first, and the first will be last' (v. 16). I hear this as Jesus' saying that a race can't be won by everyone, but everyone has his or her own race to win. We don't need to be jealous of what anyone else has, because God's generosity knows no limits. He has more than enough for everyone, and whether, in our eyes, we are more or less deserving than the person next to us, God will give to us generously just the same.

We are made in God's image (Genesis 9:6). God is beyond compare and so are we. God has made all of us in an amazing and wonderful way (Psalm 139:14). Believe that in your heart! Don't lose sight of God's plans for your life by looking at what other people are doing differently, or at what they have or don't have, and thinking you are better or worse than anyone else. These are simply distractions. Know that you are unique. You have a purpose in life unlike any other. Ask God for what you need (James 4:2); know that he is generous beyond our imagination, and trust that if at first we don't get the answer we want it's because God sees the bigger picture and knows that around the corner is something better than we could ever dream of.

TODAY'S PRACTICE

1 Find 15 minutes in your day to sit quietly, close your eyes, take in a couple of deep breaths to help you relax, and be still in the

presence of God. Imagine you are breathing in God's love and breathing out anything that is troubling you.

2 Today avoid the temptation to compare yourself with others. If you notice yourself doing it, ask God to help you focus on the many blessings he has given you, and how you can best use your energy to fulfil his unique purpose for your life.

3 At the end of the day, spend five minutes thinking about any good things that have happened and things that you have enjoyed. Fill the space for today's diary entry. Don't stop writing until the space is full. It doesn't matter how big or small the thing is that you choose to write down. All that matters is that you are noting something good that happened today. When you have written your list, thank God for all the things that are on it.

DAY 7

REFLECT ON YOUR WEEK

Come near to God and he will come near to you.

JAMES 4:8

Sometimes, especially when we are weighed down with responsibility, it can feel selfish to take time out for ourselves. Yet unless we do so, it can be easy to lose sight of who we truly are and fail to recognise any purpose to our life. Spending time in silence can help us both to get in touch with our real selves and to listen out for the still, small, voice of God in our lives and sense how he might be guiding us.

If spending time in silence is new to you, how are you finding it? Has it been difficult to fit the time into your day? Would it help to have a regular time to do this? Does morning, afternoon or evening work best for you? Starting any new routine can be difficult, so don't worry if you didn't manage to find some silent space for God each day. Instead, think about why that might be and experiment with different times and places for this special time with God, until you find something that works for you.

Looking back over the exercises in the week, were there any that you found more challenging than others? Why do you think that was? Did any experiences surprise you? Did any issues arise that you would consider significant? Are there any changes that you would like to make as a result of your experiences this week?

TODAY'S PRACTICE

1 Find 15 minutes in your day to sit quietly, close your eyes, take in a couple of deep breaths to help you relax, and be still in the presence of God. Imagine you are breathing in God's love and breathing out anything that is troubling you.

2 At the end of the day, spend five minutes thinking about any good things that have happened and things that you have enjoyed. Fill the space for today's diary entry. Don't stop writing until the space is full. It doesn't matter how big or small the thing is that you choose to write down. All that matters is that you are noting something good that happened today. When you have written your list, thank God for all the things that are on it.

WEEK 2

DO YOUR PART

You have made your way around this hill country
long enough; now turn north.

DEUTERONOMY 2:3

DAY 8

YOU HAVE A CHOICE

I have set before you life and death, blessing and curses.
Now choose life.

DEUTERONOMY 30:19

On my wall at home I have pinned the 'serenity prayer'.
Whenever I'm feeling at a loss for what to do in any situation,
I read it and let the words sink into my heart: 'God, grant me
the serenity to accept the things I cannot change, courage
to change the things I can, and the wisdom to know the
difference' (attributed to the American theologian Reinhold
Niebuhr, 1892–1971). It is a simple prayer for God's guidance,
yet it reminds me that I too have a part to play. God will
guide me, but he has given me responsibility for my own life,
and that is a great gift which is so easy to overlook.

Whenever we find ourselves in a situation we don't want
to be in, it's easy to fall into the trap of blaming other people.
How many times have you looked at circumstances in your
life and thought, if he hadn't done that…, if she had done
that…, or why has God allowed that to happen? In the past
I've even heard myself say, for example, 'If you hadn't been
talking to me when I was taking the dinner out of the oven,
then I wouldn't have burned myself.' Maybe that was true,
but what about my part? If I had been concentrating on what
I was doing and hadn't been trying to do too many things
at once, then perhaps I wouldn't have burned myself. Who
knows? Sometimes things happen to us and it's not our fault.

It may not be anyone's fault. If we keep looking to apportion blame, it's only going to stop us from finding a way out of a situation we would like to change.

A paper in Teesside I worked for for a while ran numerous stories headlined 'the war on drugs', and I interviewed many people who were addicted to heroin, most of whom had been led into a life of crime to fund their drug habit. Every person told a sad tale, but as I listened to the stories, what struck me as more upsetting was how resigned these young people were to the idea that they were helpless to lead a better life. Their stories of dysfunctional homes, abusive parents, poor schooling were so well rehearsed that I imagined they had been pitifully perfected to gain the maximum sympathy from a long list of social workers, counsellors, police, probation officers and judges.

I remember interrupting one young man as he recalled all the reasons he was in his current situation, and saying to him, 'I'm sorry you've had a hard time, but lots of people have hard lives and they don't beat and rob old ladies as you have done. You don't have to behave like that either. Whatever you think now, you're better than that.' Surprise flashed across his face as it became clear that while I was there to listen to him, I didn't want to hear the same story, with the same excuses and learned helplessness, that he'd grown accustomed to telling. I didn't want him to feel worse about himself, but neither could I condone or excuse what he had done. I wanted him to see that, given the same circumstances, someone else might have chosen to behave in a different way. Maybe he didn't have as many choices as some people had, but he did have choices, even if for a time he didn't recognise them. He also had a choice now. He could keep retelling that same story about himself and why it was inevitable that he behaved as he did, or he could try to live a new one. The sadness was that he couldn't see the possibility of any other life.

I don't know what became of that young man, but meeting him made me think about how, if we try hard enough, we can talk and reason ourselves out of, or into, doing almost anything. We may not have fallen into addiction or have committed crimes, but how many stories do we tell ourselves every day that rob us of our responsibility and stop us from moving forward, from changing a situation for the better, or from enjoying our lives?

There is a story in John's Gospel about a man who has been sick for 38 years, and although we don't know how old he is, even if he hadn't been like that his whole life, it probably felt that way to him (John 5:5). Jesus sees him lying by a pool that is said to have healing waters and asks, 'Do you want to get well?' (v. 6). Instead of saying, 'Yes,' the man does what so many of us do when we've grown used to difficult situations—he starts recalling all the reasons why he can't get well, how he doesn't have anyone to help him, and how someone always gets in the healing pool before him. It is indeed a sad story, but instead of sympathising with him, Jesus says, 'Get up! Pick up your mat, and walk' (v. 8). As he responds, immediately the man is healed; he picks up his mat and starts walking. That same man later faced criticism for carrying his mat on the sabbath (see John 5:1–14 for the full story). For me, this shows that whatever miracles God works in our lives, there will often be complications that can turn our attention in a different direction. The challenge is not to get so caught up in the complications that we fail to recognise or appreciate the miracle.

I don't know what circumstances you're facing or what

you're praying for, but whenever I have days when I feel like I've hit the bottom and just want to curl in a ball and stay down, I think about Jesus' words to that sick man. Yes, Jesus healed him, but that man had his part to play in the miracle as well. He had to believe; he had to get up; he had to pick up his mat; and he had to walk.

Today, think about your responsibility not as a burden but as a privilege. I like to think about it as God sharing his power with me, as he does with all of us through our gift of free will. Sometimes it can be difficult to see what our role may be, or perhaps even to see that we have a role to play in any given situation. In times like these I find it helps to be honest with God. Ask him to show you where you can make a difference, be open to the still small voice that guides you and, however beaten down with life you feel, know that you do have a choice. Ask for God's help, and be prepared to get up, pick up your mat and walk.

TODAY'S PRACTICE

1 Find 15 minutes in your day to sit quietly, close your eyes, take in a couple of deep breaths to help you relax, and be still in the presence of God. Imagine you are breathing in God's love and breathing out anything that is troubling you.

2 It is God's invitation to all people to join him in the ongoing creation of the world. We all have a part to play. Are you asking God to do something that you can do yourself? Think about a situation in your life, or in the world, that you would like to see changed. In your prayers ask God to show you how you can make a difference for the better. If something comes to mind, act on it. If not, be open to what that answer might be in the

coming days and weeks. It might not be what you expected but be ready to take opportunities as they arise.

3 At the end of the day, spend five minutes thinking about any good things that have happened and things that you have enjoyed. Fill the space for today's diary entry. Don't stop writing until the space is full. It doesn't matter how big or small the thing is that you choose to write down. All that matters is that you are noting something good that happened today. When you have written your list, thank God for all the things that are on it.

TAKE TIME TO REST

> God blessed the seventh day and made it holy, because on it
> he rested from all the work of creating that he had done.
> GENESIS 2:3

Kenichi Uchino was just 30 years old when he collapsed and
died on the floor of the Toyota factory where he worked as
a quality control manager. At the time of his death in 2002,
the young father of two was into his fourth hour of overtime.
For the previous six months he had routinely put in at least
80 hours of overtime per month. Kenichi had reasoned that
he needed to work such long hours in order to support his
family. Yet, because he was working 13- to 15-hour-days,
sometimes six days a week, he was too exhausted to spend
much time with them. His two children, who were aged one
and three at the time, barely recognised him as their father.

Kenichi died of sudden heart failure linked to overwork.
Sadly, he is not alone. Death from overwork is happening so
frequently that the Japanese even have a word for it, *karoshi*,
which has been legally recognised as a cause of death since
the 1980s. In China, they call it *guolaosi*, where it is thought
to claim as many as 1600 lives every day.

Asia may have recognised and named this phenomenon,
but it is not the only continent in which people are working
themselves into an early grave. In both the UK and the US
heart disease is the leading cause of death. Research published
in the British Medical Journal showed that statistically you

are more likely to have a fatal heart attack on a Monday than on any other day of the week. Studies carried out in several other countries have revealed a similar pattern. Exactly why this is, the scientists can't say, but it is thought to be linked in some way to work-related stress.

You may wonder how people allow their lives to get so out of balance that they literally end up working themselves to death. It sounds so extreme, yet there are many forms of exhaustion and burnout that creep up on us without our realising. Difficulty concentrating, physical restlessness and irritability are all signs that we need to take a break. Yet how often do we override the clear messages our bodies are giving us? Are you the person who says, 'I haven't got time to rest'? If that is you, then I hope that, even just for today, you will begin to take some time to listen to your body and recognise that there are good reasons why the Bible encourages us to rest.

I collapsed from exhaustion before I stopped taking my good health for granted and started making time for the basic building blocks of a healthy life—nutritious meals, regular exercise and restorative sleep. Everyone knows this, but we often think that we will be the one who can survive without it, and for a short while most of us can, but not long-term.

At one time I was trying to do everything—work, exercise and play—to excess, and fooled myself that I was living in balance, all the while moving further away from all the benefits I associated with a balanced life. I now realise that even in seeking balance I was somehow putting more stress on myself, because balance in life is elusive. By the nature of life our activity will tip more heavily towards one area rather than another. We may be adjusting our scales every day, but unless we decide to take care of the basic building blocks of our life, soon there will be nothing left to balance.

It is important that we work hard, but if we don't take time to rest, to step back and enjoy what we have created, how can we expect to maintain any energy and enthusiasm for life? We all have seasons in life when there are heavy demands on our time, for example, when we have a newborn baby in the house, when a relative is seriously ill, or when we're starting a new project or job. However, some people constantly live in a heightened state of feeling that they never have enough time. Is that you?

We need to realise that we can't always do everything we might plan to do, and that is OK. It took me a long time to realise that, however much I do, there will always be more to do. Rather than being a sign of failure or something to become stressed about, I've started to see it as a good thing. Rather than be weighed down by how much there is to do, I'm excited by how much there is I can do.

God never stops creating and giving us opportunities to create anew. It is how the world carries on developing and growing. In other words, we're not supposed to get it all done. Accepting that can be hard to do, but if we can, it frees us up to take time out to rest and build up our energy for the next challenge God has in store.

TODAY'S PRACTICE

1 Find 15 minutes in your day to sit quietly, close your eyes, take in a couple of deep breaths to help you relax, and be still in the presence of God. Imagine you are breathing in God's love and breathing out anything that is troubling you.

2 Are you taking time to rest and to look after your body? If you're like most people, the answer is probably, no. Many of

us have become so used to over-riding the signals our body is giving out through natural feelings of hunger and tiredness that we don't hear them properly any more. You can't change your eating, sleeping and exercise habits overnight, but you can make a decision to take a step in the right direction. The best way to make permanent lifestyle changes is to make gradual changes that become habits. Today, choose to do something that shows you care for and appreciate your health. If, like me, you have developed a habit of skipping meals or eating on the go, make time to sit down and enjoy a meal today. If you feel that you don't have time to exercise, take time out for a ten-minute-stroll to clear your head at some point during the day. If finding time to relax is problematic for you, set aside some time to do something that you find relaxing: it might be having a soak in the bath, watching your favourite TV show, or going for a run. Whatever it may be, cut yourself some slack and enjoy this time. Do your best and be content knowing that there is more to do, because the ongoing creation of the world is designed that way—it is how life should be. Taking time out to look after yourself is not selfish, it is essential. If you don't take time to look after your own health and wellbeing, soon you won't have the energy or strength to look after anyone else.

3 At the end of the day, spend five minutes thinking about any good things that have happened and things that you have enjoyed. Fill the space for today's diary entry. Don't stop writing until the space is full. It doesn't matter how big or small the thing is that you choose to write down. All that matters is that you are noting something good that happened today. When you have written your list, thank God for all the things that are on it.

WHAT IS IMPORTANT TO YOU?

For where your treasure is, there your heart will be also.
MATTHEW 6:21

There's a cartoon that got me thinking about my priorities in life. It's of a man trying to catch a wad of notes that are dangling from a fishing rod. He can almost reach the cash, but it is ever so slightly out of his grasp. He continues to chase it eagerly, his eyes focused so exclusively on the money, that he doesn't see the rod is leading him towards an open grave.

The cartoon strikes a chord in the Western world because it represents the heart of capitalism, a system driven by profits. Yet, this cartoon doesn't depict an economic system— it is of a man, and people are rarely as straightforward as academic models. Perhaps the man is chasing money so that he can add to his wealth in the bank, but more likely he is a man who wants money for what it can bring him—a better lifestyle for himself and his family, the means by which he can help someone else, or simply a bit more time to do whatever he chooses. Whatever the reason, in the race for more money the man has lost sight of what is important, and that can easily happen to any of us. Unfortunately, it's not until we're in a hole, so to speak, that many of us start to evaluate our priorities and realise what truly matters in our lives.

I was thinking about this a few months ago when I met an Indian man who works in the UK as a doctor in the emergency department. It was clear that he very much enjoyed his job. He found it exciting to work out what was wrong with a person. He viewed the diagnosis of illness as a puzzle, and got great satisfaction from being a part of helping the person to become well again. He had seen the worst of illnesses and accidents, but what upset him most was dealing with young people who had attempted to take their own lives. 'I don't understand it,' he told me. 'In India people are too busy trying to stay alive to think about killing themselves.' I don't know how true that is, but I understand his sentiment.

It is a sad fact that, even today in the 21st century, there are many people throughout the world who do not have the means to support their basic human needs, such as food, shelter and clothing. It is clear what the priorities of people in this situation are. However, once those basic needs are met, a whole new set of needs emerge. In 1943, psychologist Abraham Maslow described this development as a hierarchy of needs, in which lower level basic needs must be satisfied before we can progress to meet higher level growth needs such as safety, security, love, friendship, self-respect, autonomy and purpose.

In the years since Maslow published his motivational theory, other psychologists have suggested additional layers to the hierarchy. It's clear we humans are complex beings, so it's probably not surprising that in trying to satisfy our growing needs we get out of balance from time to time.

So often I've seen people becoming overwhelmed by the amount of things they feel they need to do. At such times it's very difficult to hear the voice of reason which says, 'If you don't like your schedule, then change it. After all, it is your schedule. God gave us all the same 1440 minutes in a day.

I know that sometimes it doesn't feel like it, but how you spend those minutes really is up to you.'

'But you don't understand,' the exhausted mind cries. 'It's a rat race out there and if I don't do all these things, I'll be left behind.'

'That may be so, but is it a race you want to be in? It sounds to me as if you're already getting trampled, and even if you do manage to stay the course and are successful, do you want to be a rat?'

Of course, no one purposely lets their life get out of balance. What is important to one person may not have the same importance to another, but when our life no longer reflects our values, then even if it doesn't affect our health immediately, it is only a matter of time before we begin to feel dissatisfied and frustrated.

The Bible tells us that wherever we put most of our time, money and energy, there we'll find our heart. Where is that place for you?

I don't know the situation you are in right now. Perhaps you are at a crossroads in your life. Maybe a crisis has forced you to re-evaluate your priorities, or perhaps everything is going well and you want to take a particular area of your life to the next level without losing the balance you've worked hard to achieve.

Wherever you find yourself at this moment, even the slightest attention to areas you may have neglected can begin to get you back on the right track. In today's exercise I want you to think about what you value most in your life. This might include your health, your family, your friends, your faith, your work, being happy, being loved, making a contribution, or achieving a goal you want to accomplish. Whatever is most important to you, write it down. You might think of lots of items, but for now, try to keep the list manageable by choosing no more than five values.

Once you have your list, think about the past week or month. What did you spend most of your time doing? Be honest with yourself! Where are your time, money and energy going? Is this where you want your heart to be? Are you making time for what matters most to you? If a complete stranger was looking at your life from the outside, would it appear that your life is a reflection of your values?

Think about one thing you can do today that will show you value what you have placed highly on your list. For example, if health is on your list, perhaps you could make sure that you eat a healthy balanced meal, or go for a brisk walk. If spending time with family is on your list, can you take time to ask your spouse about his or her day, to phone your mum or dad, or to help your child with his or her homework?

After doing the initial exercise, you might feel that you want to make some significant changes to your life. That might be necessary for you to live a life that reflects your true values, but remember that change takes time. For now, if you can take small steps towards nurturing each of your five areas, you will soon find that you are well on your way to living the life you want. Often, once you begin to make changes, the problem of what you need to stop doing or to delegate in order to find more time to do what you value most will work itself out.

TODAY'S PRACTICE

1 Find 15 minutes in your day to sit quietly, close your eyes, take in a couple of deep breaths to help you relax, and be still in the presence of God. Imagine you are breathing in God's love and breathing out anything that is troubling you.

2 List up to five things that you value most in your life. Do one thing today, no matter how small, to show that you truly value each of the points on your list.

3 At the end of the day, spend five minutes thinking about any good things that have happened and things that you have enjoyed. Fill the space for today's diary entry. Don't stop writing until the space is full. It doesn't matter how big or small the thing is that you choose to write down. All that matters is that you are noting something good that happened today. When you have written your list, thank God for all the things that are on it.

DAY 11

YOU CAN CHANGE
ONLY YOURSELF

How can you say to your brother, 'Brother, let me take the speck out of your eye,' when you yourself fail to see the plank in your own eye? You hypocrite, first take the plank out of your eye, and then you will see clearly to remove the speck from your brother's eye.

LUKE 6:42

I've heard it said many times that people never really change. I don't believe that to be true. I've seen people change for the better many times. I've seen people replace bad habits with good habits, and become healthier, calmer, kinder, more disciplined, generous, patient and loving. Changes like these rarely happen quickly or without effort, but they do happen, and more often than you might imagine. That said, I have yet to see someone change simply because someone else wanted them to behave a certain way or to hold a certain belief. I have also yet to meet someone who hasn't, at some point in their life, given changing someone else a good try.

Realising that we cannot change other people is one of the hardest lessons in life. Many times people's problems turn out to be something that is happening in someone else's life, or is due to the impact of someone else's behaviour.

Deep down we all want to be loved for who we are, but that doesn't mean those closest to us will always agree with everything we say or do. We're all unique, so we shouldn't be surprised if we rub each other up the wrong way occasionally. Usually the more time we spend with people, the more opportunity there is to find topics to disagree on or to notice habits that annoy us.

When we think about people who want to change someone else, we may imagine a person who is manipulative or controlling. Sometimes that is the case; there are some people who want to change others purely for their own benefit. Often these people won't be happy until everyone thinks like them and behaves how they would like them to behave. I've even known some who became disgruntled and took offence because their partner expressed a difference of opinion on a newspaper article. Such people will never be truly happy because, as much as they try, they will not be able to mould the rest of the world into the shape they want.

There are others, however, who genuinely want the best for the other person and believe that a change will benefit everyone involved. They are often concerned about the behaviour of an adult son or daughter, of another relative, or of a friend. If only he or she would drink less, work harder, take more interest in their children, go to church, take more exercise, quit smoking, lose weight, stop dating that person, look after themselves better, spend more time at home, go out more, be more sociable, talk less, talk more... the list goes on.

In the main these are not manipulative people. They have good hearts and mean well. When you are a caring person, it is easy to get tangled up in other people's problems and messy circumstances. Unfortunately, whatever your motivation for wanting to change someone else, you cannot, and you cannot live another person's life for them. People have the right to make their own choices in life and to make their own mistakes, as difficult as that might be to watch. Sometimes, for whatever reason, someone may even choose not to have you in their life anymore, and as hard as it may be to accept, that is also their choice.

If we're not careful, we can waste significant amounts of time and emotional energy trying to 'fix' other people, speculating on why they said what they did, worrying about what they did or didn't do, or what they meant by it, and what will happen to them if they continue as they are. When people are close to us, it is difficult to see that other people's problems are not our own, and that their responsibilities are not our responsibilities. I don't mean by this that we shouldn't help people, or provide them with opportunities to change—of course we should. What they do with those opportunities is up to them. We can offer advice; we can support people; and we can act as an example, but the decision to change has to come from within them.

TODAY'S PRACTICE

1 Find 15 minutes in your day to sit quietly, close your eyes, take in a couple of deep breaths to help you relax, and be still in the presence of God. Imagine you are breathing in God's love and breathing out anything that is troubling you.

2 Today notice if there are any times when you find yourself feeling stressed about something that is happening in someone else's life, or by something someone has said or done. It may not always be obvious that you want another person to change, so notice thoughts such as, 'I wish he wouldn't do that' or 'why can't she do this?' When you notice these thoughts, remember that God has given everyone the

freedom to be themselves and to make their own choices. Accept the person for who they are and where they are in their life right now. Think about their good qualities, pray about whatever is troubling you, and trust God to take care of the situation. Remember that you can't change other people but you can change yourself.

3 At the end of the day, spend five minutes thinking about any good things that have happened and things that you have enjoyed. Fill the space for today's diary entry. Don't stop writing until the space is full. It doesn't matter how big or small the thing is that you choose to write down. All that matters is that you are noting something good that happened today. When you have written your list, thank God for all the things that are on it.

CULTIVATE THE FRUIT OF THE SPIRIT

> Do not be deceived: God cannot be mocked. A man reaps what he sows.
>
> GALATIANS 6:7

There is a Native American story which tells of an old man talking to his grandson about the battle that goes on inside all people.

He said, 'My son, the battle is between two wolves inside us all.

'One is evil—it is anger, envy, jealousy, sorrow, regret, greed, arrogance, self-pity, guilt, resentment, inferiority, lies, false pride, superiority and ego.

'The other is good—it is joy, peace, love, hope, serenity, humility, kindness, benevolence, empathy, generosity, truth, compassion and faith.'

The grandson thought about it for a while and then asked, 'Which wolf wins?'

The old man replied, 'The one you feed.'

Which wolf are you feeding? It's not enough simply to starve the evil wolf. For the good wolf to win out, you need to feed it. Yet, when we want to change often we concentrate on things we want to stop doing, and give very little thought to what we want to be doing instead. When a teacher asks her class not to think of an elephant, what is the first image that comes to mind? You've got it—you can't 'not think of an elephant' unless you choose to think about something else instead. It's the same with any bad habit you want to break. If you keep thinking about what you shouldn't be doing, don't be surprised if you want to do it all the more.

Shaking off a bad habit or developing a good one is not easy, but neither is it beyond our ability. There is nothing mystical about a habit; it is simply a way of behaving that we have become used to by repeating it many times. If you choose to behave in a different way often enough, over time that new way of behaving will no longer feel strange because it will have become a habit.

Albert Einstein described insanity as doing the same thing over and over again and expecting different results. Basically he meant that if you keep on doing what you've always done, how can you expect your life to change?

For years scientists have attempted to determine how long it takes to break a bad habit or form a new one. In a society in which speed is everything, many were quick to jump on the view of plastic surgeon, Dr Maxwell Maltz, who, after observing patients who had undergone surgery to amputate an arm or a leg, recorded that it took about 21 days for them to stop sensing a phantom limb. He noticed that in his own life too, it took him about the same length of time to get used to a new situation, for example feeling comfortable in a new home, and therefore, he concluded, changing a mental image takes a minimum of 21 days.[6]

More recently, researchers from University College London suggested that it takes an average of 66 days to change a habit, but participants in the study took anywhere from 18 to 254 days.[7] Results also showed that it doesn't matter if people slipped up now and again in their new regime. Missing an opportunity to do the new behaviour didn't significantly impact on the process of change, although people who were very inconsistent in performing the behaviour did not succeed in creating new habits.

The key here is about being consistent. It doesn't matter if you can form a habit in 18 days or if you're still struggling 200 days later. Most people who successfully change their behaviour have tried many times before they succeed. All that matters is that we get ourselves on the right track and keep moving in the direction we want to go. Even when we think we've failed, if we get ourselves back on track again we will eventually succeed. If you think about it in terms of feeding the good wolf, it's not something that we do for a time and then stop. The wolf needs feeding with good nourishing food, regularly, for the rest of our lives.

Most people think about habits in the context of behaviours that are harmful to health and wellbeing such as smoking, drug addiction, excessive alcohol intake or overeating. If you have this type of habit, it is good to get some help and advice about it, because there is lots of specialist support available that can get you on the right road. However, while bad habits may be more obvious, most of our behaviour is habitual; we just don't always see it that way.

Today our exercise is about developing good habits. Paul invites us to be sensitive to the Spirit in us and says that those who allow themselves to be guided by the Spirit will be recognised by the fruits of love, joy, peace, forbearance (patience), kindness, goodness, faithfulness, gentleness and self-control, that grow in their lives (Galatians 5:22–23). You can't cultivate these fruits simply by deciding that you want to be patient, loving or joyful. The fruits will grow in our lives through practice, and we need to keep feeding and nourishing these traits until they become a natural part of who we are. You might think, 'Oh well, it's my nature. I'm just an impatient person, or I'm just not very enthusiastic, peaceful, compassionate', or whatever it may be. Does that reflect the image of God? The Spirit has sowed the seeds of a better, healthier and happier life within you, and if you ask for help, God will give you the strength to change.

TODAY'S PRACTICE

1 Find 15 minutes in your day to sit quietly, close your eyes, take in a couple of deep breaths to help you relax, and be still in the presence of God. Imagine you are breathing in God's love and breathing out anything that is troubling you.

2 Today, notice which wolf you are feeding. Start nourishing love, joy, peace, patience, kindness, goodness, faithfulness, gentleness and self-control in your life. Recognise that cultivating the fruits of the Spirit takes practice, and see difficulties as opportunities to help you to develop and grow. Know this is not something to do for a season—it is a way of life. If you fall down sometimes, that's fine. Just get back up and ask God for help to keep going. Whenever you find yourself stumbling, remind yourself that you're still heading in the right direction and, although you might not be where you aim to be, you are further on than you were at the start.

3 At the end of the day, spend five minutes thinking about any good things that have happened and things that you have enjoyed. Fill the space for today's diary entry. Don't stop writing until the space is full. It doesn't matter how big or small the thing is that you choose to write down. All that matters is that you are noting something good that

happened today. When you have written your list, thank God for all the things that are on it.

DAY 13

WHAT ARE YOU WAITING FOR?

Whoever watches the wind will not plant; whoever looks at the clouds will not reap.

ECCLESIASTES 11:4

I've always enjoyed stories and I've always enjoyed writing. Recently, when I was clearing out some old papers in my office I came across some of the writing I did when I was at school. When I was about 13 years old, I got involved in a new community magazine for young people called *Off the Wall*. It was a fantastic experience, and I discovered that I really enjoyed interviewing people and writing articles. I got to interview local singers and business people. I even managed to get an interview with the late Dudley Moore, which amazes me now, looking back, and I'm grateful for his encouragement at such a young age.

I've since interviewed several Hollywood stars, and I now realise just how special it was that Dudley Moore responded positively to my request. Even well-established publications with large readerships can struggle to secure high profile interviews, and here was I, a school girl, writing for a small, local publication, which back then couldn't even extend its readership with the internet. Of course, I didn't think about that at the time. I just thought, 'Who would I like to interview?'

When we published our magazine, I was interviewed by a reporter from the regional newspaper in the area and another from a local radio station about how I'd managed to get the story. At the time I didn't understand the interest or the questions they asked me. To me, at the time, there was nothing complicated about it. I wanted to interview Dudley Moore, so I asked and he said, 'Yes.'

As an adult such thinking seems naïve. How could I have thought life was so straightforward? But was it really that my life became more complicated, or was it simply that I became more aware of the obstacles? I would think about why I wanted to do something, but then I'd come up with ten more reasons why I couldn't do it, or at least why it would be difficult, or why I couldn't do it right now. Instead of just starting anything, I began to look too far ahead.

At university I met a guy to whom I was really attracted and we went on a few dates. He was a couple of years older than me and talked a lot about how he planned to go travelling around the world for a year when he graduated, which was only a few months away. I decided that I didn't want to get involved. I don't think I gave a reason at the time, but I know that it was because I was afraid of getting hurt by giving my heart to someone who was going to be out of the country for a year at least. When I was 19 years old, a year seemed an awfully long time. Fast-forward a few years and the same guy was still living in the city and had not yet set off on his huge global adventure. Meanwhile, I was in a relationship with a man whose work took him out of the country, sometimes for months at a time. There was a lesson in there somewhere about listening to my heart as well as my head, but it would take me much longer to recognise, and longer still to start learning it.

For many years my life became more complicated than it needed to be. I had dreams of writing books but, as life has a habit of throwing up tasks that need to be done more urgently, it was always something that I was going to do at some time in the future when I had more time. Instead of thinking about the writing part of it, which I enjoyed, I was concentrating on the finished product and I was getting overwhelmed. I didn't see how I could write anything worthwhile in the short spaces of time I had available, so outside of my job as a newspaper journalist I wrote nothing at all.

So what changed? Well, I didn't suddenly get a windfall cheque to allow me to leave the day job, a flash of inspiration or any major changes to my circumstances, but I did meet someone who was writing books successfully already. I was working as a feature writer at the time on the *Manchester Evening News*, and I was asked to interview the crime writer Val McDermid. It was a job I was pleased to take, not only because I was interested to talk to her about her early career in journalism and how she had made the move to become a full-time author, but also because she has a second home on the Northumberland coast, and that would be my dream writing retreat.

We met for a late breakfast at a café near where she lives. After the initial introductions, I complimented her. I told her that she was living my dream life. How amazing must it be to look out to sea and write! I thought that she might say, 'Thank you,' and tell me how much she enjoyed mulling over her characters while on long coastal walks. Not a bit. She simply replied, quite matter of fact, 'Well, what are you waiting for? Stop talking about it and just do it.' At the time I thought her response was a bit harsh, but it was the best advice she could have given me, because I did just that. I realised, as the Bible says, that if I always waited for perfect weather with no clouds, I would never reap the harvest I wanted. Less than two years later, I had a completed manuscript and a publishing contract. It wasn't a new idea. It was one I had been playing around with in my head for at least ten years. What had changed? I was no longer waiting for perfect circumstances. Instead of focusing on what I couldn't do, I decided to take action and do what I could.

Is there something you've been putting off? Do you find yourself saying, 'I'll get round to it tomorrow', or 'When I've got more time', 'When work settles down', or 'When the children have left home', or 'When I've retired', or simply, 'Later'? Like the Chinese philosopher, Lao Tzu said, 'A journey of a thousand miles begins with a single step.' What is stopping you from taking that first step right now?

TODAY'S PRACTICE

1 Find 15 minutes in your day to sit quietly, close your eyes, take in a couple of deep breaths to help you relax, and be still in the presence of God. Imagine you are breathing in God's love and breathing out anything that is troubling you. Chose a word or phrase that is comforting for you and repeat it gently in your mind. Examples you might want to try are: *maranatha*; I am filled with the healing love of God; I can do all things through Christ who strengthens me. If your thoughts wander, don't worry about this—it is normal. Simply notice it and bring your thoughts back to your chosen word or phrase.

2 Today focus on what you can do instead of what you can't. Start with something small. For example, if you would like to live in a more peaceful world, start by bringing peace to those around you with a smile, kind words or actions. If you would

like to see more harmony in your home, if the washing-up needs doing or the rubbish needs emptying and you can do it, then don't wait to be asked or until it's your turn, just do it. If you haven't got time to travel to visit a friend or relative you've been meaning to see, could you pick up the phone to ask how they are? If there is a project you've been meaning to get around to, is there something you can do to make a start? Whatever it is you have been putting off, make a start today. Don't worry about obstacles because they will show up as they do for everyone. Ask for God's help and trust that once you take the first step, he will guide you to the next.

3 At the end of the day, spend five minutes thinking about any good things that have happened and things that you have enjoyed. Fill the space for today's diary entry. Don't stop writing until the space is full. It doesn't matter how big or small the thing is that you choose to write down. All that matters is that you are noting something good that happened today. When you have written your list, thank God for all the things that are on it.

DAY 14

REFLECT ON YOUR WEEK

I know your deeds. See, I have placed before you an open door that no one can shut.

REVELATION 3:8

When life gets tough, the choices we have can appear blurred. Indeed, it can often feel as though we have no choice at all. However, whatever situation we find ourselves in, we always have choices, even if it is simply the choice to live with a different attitude. Sometimes our situation is simply due to a habit that we have become so used to that we now think of it as part of who we are. It is never easy to change habits or attitudes. It takes time and persistence, but the start of any change is recognising that we have some part to play in making it happen. Ask God to help you see yourself as you really are; to make your choices more visible; and to give you the strength to act on the ones that seem right for you at this time, so that you are living a life that reflects your values better.

Looking back over the exercises in the week, were there any that you found more challenging than others? Why do you think that was? Did any experiences surprise you? Did any issues arise that you would consider significant? Are there any changes that you would like to make as a result of your experiences this week?

Did you spend some time in silence each day? If you didn't, what do you think is preventing you from spending this time with God? Recognise the difference between genuine reasons and excuses you tell yourself. If you have a genuine reason, could you look to incorporate this time into your life in a different way?

TODAY'S PRACTICE

1 Find 15 minutes in your day to sit quietly, close your eyes, take in a couple of deep breaths to help you relax, and be still in the presence of God. Imagine you are breathing in God's love and breathing out anything that is troubling you.

2 At the end of the day, spend five minutes thinking about any good things that have happened and things that you have enjoyed. Fill the space for today's diary entry. Don't stop writing until the space is full. It doesn't matter how big or small the thing is that you choose to write down. All that matters is that you are noting something good that happened today. When you have written your list, thank God for all the things that are on it.

WEEK 3

LET GO

Make sure that nobody pays back wrong for wrong,
but always strive to do what is good for each other
and for everyone else.

1 THESSALONIANS 5:15

DAY 15

FORGIVE

Get rid of all bitterness, rage and anger, brawling and slander, along with every form of malice. Be kind and compassionate to one another, forgiving each other, just as in Christ God forgave you.

EPHESIANS 4:31–32

Ray Rossiter was just 20 years old when he was captured by Japanese soldiers during World War II and held as a Far Eastern Prisoner of War (FEPOW). Like Eric Lomax, whose story was told in the film *The Railway Man*, Ray was one of the soldiers to survive the building of the Burma railway, known as the railway of death because it claimed 393 lives for every mile of track laid.

Both men's capacity to forgive what happened during those three-and-a-half years is astonishing and doesn't sit easily with our natural instinct for justice. In many ways it would be easier to understand if they had become locked in bitterness, fear and vengeance after the horrors they witnessed. How could anyone forgive such brutality? When I asked Ray this question, he simply said, 'I'm a Christian and that's what we're taught to do.'

Being a Christian myself, I was sure it wasn't that straightforward. Yet over time I've come to understand Ray's answer a little more. Being a Christian for Ray isn't the same as saying he was a tax inspector or a soldier. It is not a compartment of his life, labelled 'religion'. It's a way of life that defines who he is, and because of that he lives with a forgiving spirit.

As Christians we talk about forgiveness all the time. It's a central teaching of the faith and is right there at the centre of the Lord's Prayer: 'Forgive us our trespasses as we forgive those who trespass against us'. Indeed, the words are so familiar that it's easy to say them without thinking about what they mean when lived out. We can talk about forgiveness as an abstract concept, and it all sounds very good, but it doesn't touch our hearts. When we actually witness forgiveness lived out, like in Ray's example, it is life-changing. That's why people like the late Nelson Mandela were so admired throughout the world. He wasn't simply talking the Christian message—he was living it. Of course, Ray doesn't pretend forgiving was easy. Like he says in his naturally understated way, 'It took a bit of doing.'

At the time the Japanese army had no concept of honourable surrender, so they had nothing but contempt for the soldiers imprisoned and didn't observe the Geneva Convention with regard to prisoners' care.

I asked Ray how he managed to keep his faith in such appalling circumstances. He said, 'I felt that God was there all the time, his love shining through the actions of men, one for another. He was there in every kindness, every act of compassion. This is how we survived. It was often said: "It is every man for himself in here," but in reality nothing was further from the truth. We depended so much on one another for encouragement, morale boosting, and in numerous instances for our very survival.'

I like the idea that kindness is necessary to our very survival. It made me think about how many small acts of kindness and courtesy we take for granted every day and how we can so easily overlook the significance of these small gestures in enriching our lives. Yet, in those prisoner of war camps, when every dignity was stripped away, the smallest of kindnesses shone through and were never forgotten.

While most of us will never endure such experiences, we all have an incident or period in our life that we wish had worked out differently or had never happened at all. It's become common for people to describe anything from the most terrible crimes to a cross word between friends as being unforgivable, when perhaps what they really mean is that the consequences of what has been done or said can't be erased. To 'forgive and forget' is a myth that sadly prevents many of us from looking to the future with hope.

By forgiving Ray wasn't condoning or belittling the atrocities of the camps, and he never forgot what happened. At the same time he knew that allowing hatred to fester could only lead to more pain. As he said, 'The happiest people are those who can find it in their hearts to forgive.'

When Ray explained forgiveness this way it made me think that following Jesus' example of forgiveness, however difficult it might feel at times, is a better way to live, and it is essential if we are to enjoy our lives, and enjoy them to the full.

Ray learned this through experience, but the last 30 years have seen a growing body of scientific evidence pointing the same way. The United Nations' report *Forgiveness* cites psychological studies which suggest that a forgiving attitude improves physical and mental health, and makes us feel stronger by restoring a sense of personal power and control. Controlled tests have shown that forgiveness can reduce anxiety and depression, and improve hope and self-esteem. Letting go of old hurts has also been shown to have a positive impact on heart health, to improve blood pressure, to reduce stress and to boost immunity.

We can speculate forever about why things happen or why some people do terrible deeds, but we rarely find the answers we seek. I can't begin to understand what Ray went through in those camps, but the goodness he reflects through his capacity to forgive makes me want to live a better life, and science is proving that his choice is better and healthier for us too. Life can be messy, but we are all given choices every day—to forgive or not, to let go of pain or to let it weigh heavy in our hearts. In choosing to forgive we are choosing to love, and to live the best life we can today.

TODAY'S PRACTICE

1 Find 15 minutes in your day to sit quietly, close your eyes, take in a couple of deep breaths to help you relax, and be still in the presence of God. Imagine you are breathing in God's love and breathing out anything that is troubling you.

2 Today recognise any areas of resentment in your heart and bring to mind any people you need to forgive. Decide, as a gift to yourself, to forgive and to let go of any thoughts of revenge or outward signs of bitterness, anger or malice. Ask for God's help and trust him to heal you. When we've been hurt, forgiving can feel very uncomfortable, so don't worry if you feel that there is someone in your life whom you are struggling to forgive. Be gentle with yourself, knowing that wanting to forgive is a step in itself.

3 At the end of the day, spend five minutes thinking about any good things that have happened and things that you have enjoyed. Fill the space for today's diary entry. Don't stop

writing until the space is full. It doesn't matter how big or small the thing is that you choose to write down. All that matters is that you are noting something good that happened today. When you have written your list, thank God for all the things that are on it.

DAY 16

START AFRESH

I, even I, am he who blots out your transgressions, for my own sake, and remembers your sins no more.
ISAIAH 43:25

There was a time when it was compulsory in most English towns to have a bull baited before it was slaughtered by a butcher. It was also common to bleed turkeys to death by making a small cut to their mouth and hanging them upside down, nail geese to the floor, and whip calves and pigs to death with knotted ropes. It's hard to imagine these days that such rituals were not judged to be cruel. Some of this behaviour was justified by the idea of human supremacy over animals, but there was also a belief that pain was an inevitable part of life, something that could not be controlled and so had to be faced with equanimity. As it became clear, with improvements in medicine, that pain could be relieved, cruelty became defined through pain, and ideas of what was acceptable treatment of all living beings began to change.

In 1776 an Anglican priest, Humphrey Primatt, opened the discussion in England on animal rights writing, 'Pain is pain, whether it is inflicted on man or on beast; and the creature that suffers it, whether man or beast, being sensible of the misery of it whilst it lasts, suffers evil.'[8] Pity, compassion and a reluctance to inflict pain became seen as civilised emotions, a move that improved not just animal rights, but also treatment of marginalised groups, such as those who had committed crimes or who were mentally ill.

When people realised that pain wasn't a force beyond their control and that they had a part to play in it, they also began to feel a sense of guilt at inflicting pain. Acting on this guilt led to a change in consciousness and better conditions for people and animals alike. Looking at it in this way, guilt can be seen as a valuable, healthy and creative emotion. It makes us sensitive to suffering in the world and aware of our own responsibility, reminding us that our actions are not predetermined. We have choices. We are not controlled by our circumstances, by our past, or by forces too powerful to resist. Guilt protects us in all our relationships—with ourselves, with others and with God. If we recognise that we've done wrong, we can show remorse, apologise and change our behaviour.

How have we turned what essentially is a healthy and necessary emotion into one of life's great burdens that, instead of bringing us closer to God and other people, pushes us further away? This is the unhealthy emotion we've come to associate more familiarly with guilt. It is an emotion that doesn't lead us to repent and seek forgiveness. It doesn't help us to change, but instead leaves us feeling condemned. There is nothing creative about this kind of unhealthy guilt. It's oppressive and stifling. It leaves an indelible mark on the psyche—'I am no good'—and deprives us of any joy. Such a belief can lead to hopelessness and despair, a deep sadness that penetrates a person's whole existence, which is often alleviated temporarily by projecting it on to others, causing more pain. Sadly so many people fall into this way of thinking without even recognising it. It's like a bad atmosphere that we can't see, yet when we're in it we instinctively know that something is wrong.

This kind of unhealthy guilt is often irrational and can be attached to all kinds of situations. Have you ever felt that whatever you're doing, you really ought to be doing something else, somewhere else? It reminds me of the old saying: time you enjoy wasting is not wasted time. How many of us live like that? If we always think that we should be doing something else, are we really enjoying our life or simply enduring it?

Of course, there will be times in all of our lives when we feel that we've made a mess of a situation and there may be nothing we can do to change it. We aren't free to ignore the results of our actions; we have to live with the consequences. We don't have to pretend that we are not hurting if we are, but neither do we have to live under condemnation. However big our sins are, God's love is greater. No matter who we are or what we've done, God does not reject us. The challenge is to accept ourselves as we are and not as we would like to be.

The Bible says, 'There is now no condemnation for those who are in Christ Jesus' (Romans 8:1). God isn't totting up a long list of every mistake you've ever made. He is there to heal, not punish. His focus is on what you're doing right, not what you're doing wrong. You may not feel worthy of this love and mercy, but none of us are. In turning to God for forgiveness, our unworthiness leads us to a life of humility rather than shame. Like Jesus said to those about to stone a woman to death for committing adultery, 'Let any one of you who is without sin be the first to throw a stone at her' (John 8:7). This doesn't mean that we accept our sin, but we accept ourselves, and know that we are not our sin. We are made in the image of God and however bad we feel at any one moment, we have the capacity for good within us.

Focus on that goodness, on your qualities rather than on your defects. We've all made mistakes. We need to learn from mistakes, not be defined by them. It doesn't do you or anyone else any good to keep putting yourself down. Your future is open, and although that may seem hard to accept, if you turn to God for forgiveness he will restore the strength and courage you need to move forward with hope.

TODAY'S PRACTICE

1 Find 15 minutes in your day to sit quietly, close your eyes, take in a couple of deep breaths to help you relax, and be still in the presence of God. Imagine you are breathing in God's love and breathing out anything that is troubling you.

2 Are there any areas in your life where you are holding on to unhealthy guilt? Write down what you did that you feel guilty about. It will hurt to recall these things, but don't worry, that is a natural reaction and it is how we learn not to repeat the same mistakes again. Think about what you have learned and how you will change your behaviour from today. In prayer ask for God's forgiveness. Ask if there is anything you can do to make amends. Sometimes there won't be, but if you can apologise to someone you have hurt, do so, without expecting anything in return. Ask for God's healing and for the courage to learn from your mistakes. Destroy the piece of paper you've written, knowing you are graciously and generously forgiven, and that God keeps no record of your sins.

3 At the end of the day, spend five minutes thinking about any good things that have happened and things that you have enjoyed. Fill the space for today's diary entry. Don't stop writing until the space is full. It doesn't matter how big or

small the thing is that you choose to write down. All that matters is that you are noting something good that happened today. When you have written your list, thank God for all the things that are on it.

BE THE PEACEMAKER

If it is possible, as far as it depends on you, live at peace
with everyone.
ROMANS 12:18

Do you sometimes think that it would be easy to live a
peaceful life if it wasn't for all the other people who cause
havoc and disruption around you? At times like these, when
we are caught up in the detail of our everyday interactions, it
can be hard to believe that our lives would be more peaceful
if we could learn to overlook little slights and quickly forgive
offences. Somehow that sounds so simple. Yet, just because
something is straightforward doesn't mean that it is always
easy for us to do.

Jesus warns us about judging our brother for a speck
of dust in his eye, while ignoring the plank in our own
(Matthew 7:3), and, in Ephesians, Paul urges us not to go
to bed angry (Ephesians 4:6). For many of us these Bible
passages have become so familiar that it is easy to overlook
the wisdom in them. What would it look like for us truly to
live in this way?

Today our exercise encourages us to live with a more
forgiving spirit. We may not always consciously recognise
it as such, but we forgive people all the time, because no
human relationship can survive without it. It's a challenge
we all face to a greater or lesser extent, but one we often
don't think about deeply until something major happens

in our life. Thinking about forgiveness on a grand scale, as something that only amazing and selfless people are able to do, makes it easier to ignore the many areas of life where we could learn to be more forgiving every day. Yes, God's grace is in forgiveness, but what about our part? What can we do to nurture a more forgiving spirit, to be more peaceful, and to keep our hearts open so that we are able to recognise and benefit from all the good that God is doing in our lives?

Our neighbourhood, church and work place are all areas which challenge us to live in harmony with people of all ages; people who will often have different personalities, needs, priorities and sometimes different values to us. This can be especially challenging in the work place where you can spend a large part of your day with people you might never choose to spend time with otherwise. Whatever your job, there will be pressures to get it done well and on time, and unfortunately there will be people who, at times, feel like more of a hindrance than a help.

For me, one the best parts of working as a journalist is the variety of people I meet in all kinds of situations. Unfortunately, there are some who have already decided that all journalists are sour people who only want to tell the worst of life. It's fine if someone doesn't want to talk to me, but often these same people feel the need to be very vocal about it. Even in social situations they will make it clear that they don't want to speak to me in case I write about them, yet take umbrage when I do what they ask and ignore them. Faced with such hostility it would be easy to become cynical, to forget that these people are a noisy minority, and to begin to act in the underhand manner they expect. But would that make me feel better about myself and would it help me enjoy my job?

It's always upsetting when people assume the worst of you, whoever they may be. Sometimes you don't have to do anything wrong for people to decide they don't like you. There are those who will accuse you of looking at them the wrong way, when you weren't even aware you were looking in their direction. Some will find a reason to dislike you because you are different to them, in whatever way. I've even heard people being criticised because they are too nice! Trying to make everyone like or agree with you is one of the surest ways to lose your peace of mind. You can't change how people react to you, but you can change how you respond to them. You can do your part, and think, as Paul asks, about whether you are trying to please people or to do right by God (Galatians 1:10).

Each person is made in the image of God. Yes, even that person who appears to get up in the morning just to annoy you. When dealing with somebody difficult, it can help to remember this, because it changes our perspective and forces us to look for the good, to give a person the benefit of the doubt, and not to make negative assumptions. There are circumstances, however, when a person pushes our buttons so many times and so hard that it can be very difficult to see any good in them at all.

At times like these I like to think of them in the same way that the Lakota people of North America think about the Heyoka members of their tribe. The Heyoka are jesters, sometimes called sacred clowns, whose job it is purposefully to turn the world upside down. So, they might ride on a horse backwards, complain about how full they are when people are hungry, or shiver with cold when the weather is baking hot. By being irritants on purpose, they challenge people to stop taking themselves so seriously and to stop taking the actions of other people personally. They remind their people that they can't escape annoyances and problems in their lives, but they can learn to react to them in a different way.

If we base our peace on our circumstances, we will always find something or someone to upset us. Don't bicker about what doesn't really matter. There are enough troubles in life without looking for more. Decide today that you won't allow yourself to get caught up in other people's chaos, or allow other people to distract you from the good that God is working in your life. Don't wait for others to change until you can feel at peace; peace starts with you.

TODAY'S PRACTICE

1   Find 15 minutes in your day to sit quietly, close your eyes, take in a couple of deep breaths to help you relax, and be still in the presence of God. Imagine you are breathing in God's love and breathing out anything that is troubling you.

2   Today see if you can go through the day without making any negative assumptions about a person or situation. Choose to see the best in people, rather than to focus on their bad points, and use anyone who brings chaos to your day as an opportunity to practise letting go of minor irritations and forgiving quickly.

3   At the end of the day, spend five minutes thinking about any good things that have happened and things that you have enjoyed. Fill the space for today's diary entry. Don't stop writing until the space is full. It doesn't matter how big or small the thing is that you choose to write down. All that matters is that you are noting something good that happened today. When you have written your list, thank God for all the things that are on it.

IT'S NOT TOO LATE

'For I know the plans I have for you,' declares the Lord,
'plans to prosper you and not to harm you, plans to give you
hope and a future.'

JEREMIAH 29:11

Have you ever spent time wishing your circumstances
were how they had been at some point in the past? Or has
something so life-changing happened that you feel not only
that things can never be the same again, but also that life
can never be good again? Whether we are 25 years old or
75 years old, there are times when we can all feel that we've
missed our chance, that it's too late. However, there are
examples all around us of people who felt this way and then
life turned out differently.

One of my greatest lessons in how God not only changes
hearts but gives us the strength to build a new life, better
than anything anyone could have imagined, came from
a woman who was half a century older than me called
Mary Butterwick. When Mary's husband, John, died after
a very short illness, her world was thrown into turmoil.[9]
Bereavement can lead to a time of self-pity, as Mary
discovered, and there were moments when she contemplated
suicide. She felt no one knew the depth of her grief and that
her life would not only never be the same again, but that it
could never be good again. Her loss was magnified by the
lack of care that she witnessed in the two weeks between

John taking ill and dying—unkind words and neglectful treatment by one or two hospital staff that she couldn't get out of her mind.

Mary had known hard times—she had lived through the Great Depression of the 1930s and World War II. However, she couldn't cope with the lack of caring she now saw in the world, especially for those who were at the end of their lives, who she felt were being discarded as if they were already dead. In her frustration and grief Mary questioned God. 'Why John? Why did he die in this way? Where is the care, where is the love, where are you, God? Where are you in all of this mess?' She had so much she wanted to know, about death, dying and the afterlife. Mary didn't always find the answers she thought she was seeking. Sometimes she found only more questions, but in her searching she opened up a conversation with God.

In her prayers Mary admitted to God that she didn't have it all together. She had serious deep wounds that she didn't know how to heal. Jesus said, 'Come to me, all you who are weary and burdened, and I will give you rest' (Matthew 11:28). Mary felt heavy laden and she was crying out for his help.

Each lunchtime when she got home from the tea factory where she worked, Mary would sit at the table with a hot drink and read a passage from the Bible. At the same time she asked God to open her heart to take whatever she needed from the reading.

Although she wasn't aware of it at the time, Mary was inviting the Holy Spirit to guide her. In her quiet prayer time she was allowing her soul to listen, her heart to open and her spirit to grow.

In time, Mary began to forgive but she couldn't forget

the unnecessary pain caused by neglect. She believed that there had to be a better way to help families facing a similar situation; she just didn't know how to find it.

Mary initially felt hopeless, but then she realised that whenever she felt that there was nothing she could do, of course there was something: she could pray.

One day after her daily prayer time, Mary felt an urge to write. She began writing about a house where care and love are valued above all, a place where those who couldn't be physically healed would leave feeling better in mind and spirit.

Mary was not an educated or a wealthy woman. At 54 years old, she thought no one would listen to her unless she stepped out in faith and showed them what good care could look like. So, Mary sold her bungalow to buy a more suitable house to open as a day care centre. In doing so she faced opposition from doctors who believed she was meddling in areas she knew nothing about and from others who dismissed it as an utopian dream which could never work. But Mary didn't worry about what other people had to say about her dream; she listened to what God had put on her heart and trusted that if she did what she could, God would do the rest.

Today Butterwick Hospice Care helps up to 200 patients and their families each day, with three dedicated adult hospice units and a children's unit. And at the age of 90, Mary could still be found in one or other of the buildings, helping out by spending time with patients, promoting the work of the hospice and organising the annual thanksgiving service. She died in 2015, aged 91, in the hospice she had founded.

So often we tell ourselves that if only we had more

money, power, knowledge or influential friends, then we could really make a difference. Mary Butterwick had none of those things. At the time when she started campaigning for better palliative care, Mary was at an age when most people are thinking about retirement, or at least thinking they are too old to start something new. She didn't have any formal education and worked part-time in a tea factory. She had no medical background and no friends in high places, but she believed in the power of love, recognised the importance of our smallest actions and had the strength to speak her mind and take action against injustice.

We all have a role in the world but sometimes we get knocked back and think that our best times are behind us, or that we've missed out on our chances. We can all dwell on paths in life that we didn't take, but that doesn't help us to live in the best way possible here today. We can reflect, but we can't turn back. Sometimes, like Mary in her bereavement, we know that life will never be the same again, but as it changes, life can become good again. If we spend our energy wishing everything were how it used to be, we won't have the energy for the new ventures God has in store for us. Don't believe people who discourage you and tell you that you are too old, not qualified or haven't got what it takes. We've all got what it takes to fulfil God's plan for our lives and his work for us is never done—there is always someone to care for, someone to help and someone to love.

TODAY'S PRACTICE

1 Find 15 minutes in your day to sit quietly, close your eyes, take in a couple of deep breaths to help you relax, and be still in the

presence of God. Imagine you are breathing in God's love and breathing out anything that is troubling you.

2 Today if you are tempted to spend time wishing things were how they used to be, bring your thoughts back to what you are doing right now, in the moment, and ask God to show you the opportunities available to you. Notice if you are holding on to a false belief about yourself that is stopping you from pursuing a dream that God has placed in your heart. Decide to shake off any discouragement and do what you can, trusting that once you've made a start, God will show you the way.

3 At the end of the day, spend five minutes thinking about any good things that have happened and things that you have enjoyed. Fill the space for today's diary entry. Don't stop writing until the space is full. It doesn't matter how big or small the thing is that you choose to write down. All that matters is that you are noting something good that happened today. When you have written your list, thank God for all the things that are on it.

DAY 19

GOD HAS NO LIMITS

And we know that in all things God works for the good of those who love him, who have been called according to his purpose.

ROMANS 8:28

Have you ever worked for someone who wasn't happy for you to get on and do a good job, but instead insisted that whatever needed to be done was carried out in a particular way, namely the way they would do it? Annoying, isn't it? It can feel as if you are working with one hand tied behind your back, because if there is only one way you are allowed to complete a task, this becomes restrictive. Of course, there are precision jobs for which correct procedures need to be followed. Usually, however, if you want everyone to do everything exactly the way you want it to be done, you're setting yourself up for disappointment, and won't enjoy the best of another person in any relationship. As my dad would say, 'If you want something doing exactly the way you would do it, then do it yourself.' In the end, that is a lonely and tiring way to live.

It's easy to get irritated when someone forces their expectations on us, but not so easy to manage our own expectations of others and even our expectations of God. Have you ever had a sinking feeling in your stomach when life doesn't go as planned and someone says, 'Don't worry. I'm sure it will all turn out for the best'? When facing disappointment, it is hard to see how any good can come from not getting what we want, when we want it. This is where faith steps in. We might not always be able to see how it could be possible for a situation to turn out well, but we need to know deep in our hearts that all things work together for good. It's often many years later before I can see why something I thought was ideal for me wouldn't have been good for me at all. If we look back on our lives, we will all be able to find examples of this, even when, as with Joseph in the Old Testament, other people did something with the intention of harming us and God turned the situation around and used it for good (Genesis 50:20).

Help doesn't always come from the expected places, and sometimes it is only with hindsight that we can recognise the positive influence of people and events in our lives. If we continue to stay upset because events haven't gone a certain way, or because one person hasn't met our needs in ways we hoped, are we putting limits on God? Are we closing our eyes to other ways he might be working in our lives, and to people and circumstances he might bring across our path to fulfil our needs in other ways?

One of the best examples I've heard to illustrate unanswered prayer came from Fritz Kunkel, a medical doctor and psychologist who turned to psychotherapy after losing an arm while working as a medical officer on the front line in World War I. Kunkel told a story about a businessman who is praying that the bank will give him a loan before his creditors force him into bankruptcy. The man lays the whole situation out before God—how he needs the loan in order for his business to be saved, how he needs the money from the business to educate his children, and how his wife would not be able to survive should his business fail. In short, he would lose everything. He feels sure that God will intervene and change the mind of the bank manager, but when he goes to the bank, his loan is refused and as a result his business is forced to close. The man is in despair. He knows himself to be a good, honest man. How could God allow this to happen? How could God not answer his prayer?

The man finds another job, but there is much less money coming into the family home and he can't afford to go out and socialise in the evenings in the way he used to. Through the wall he hears his wife crying because of what their life has become, and he wishes he could die. It is at this low point that he takes out the watercolour paints he'd bought as a student. Those were happy times! At first painting becomes a way to bury his sorrows, but after a while the activity becomes an expression of joy. He continues in his job, but in time his painting grows until he becomes well known for his art. He's not making a fortune, but he feels happier, and his joy reflects on to all he meets. His wife learns to be more self-sufficient and recognises the benefits of living with a contented man. His children change too. Their father isn't the harassed, frustrated man they once knew. He is well adjusted and wise. His painting brings him a satisfaction he'd never known before, so he no longer tries to live his life through his children's achievements and allows them to follow their own dreams. Although the man didn't recognise it for many years, the prayer he thought had gone unanswered was to teach him what he needed, and didn't even know he had to learn.

TODAY'S PRACTICE

1 Find 15 minutes in your day to sit quietly, close your eyes, take in a couple of deep breaths to help you relax, and be still in the presence of God. Imagine you are breathing in God's love and breathing out anything that is troubling you.

2 Often we aren't aware of how many expectations we place on other people, on our circumstances and even on ourselves. Today, notice any times when you become uptight, disappointed or upset because life doesn't go as planned. Know that there is always more than one way to achieve any goal in life, and let go of any expectations that are holding you back and causing you to close your eyes to where God is opening up new opportunities in your life.

3 At the end of the day, spend five minutes thinking about any good things that have happened and things that you have enjoyed. Fill the space for today's diary entry. Don't stop writing until the space is full. It doesn't matter how big or small the thing is that you choose to write down. All that matters is that you are noting something good that happened today. When you have written your list, thank God for all the things that are on it.

DAY 20

TRUST GOD

Cast your cares on the Lord and he will sustain you.

PSALM 55:22

'Give it to God,' is a common phrase used among Christians when talking about their troubles. As I was a natural worrier when I was younger, this was a phrase I found difficult to understand and even more difficult to put into practice. What exactly did it mean when people said, 'Give it to God'? Did it mean pray about it, or was it simply a cop-out, shorthand for burying my head in the sand and doing nothing?

Not really knowing what it meant, I'd pray about whatever was troubling me and then I'd stay up all night worrying as well. I'd try to force situations one way or another, even if it meant the outcome wasn't in my favour—anything in order to create certainty! The problem is that we can't have absolute certainty in all areas of life, so to live chasing certainty was only leading me to feel more anxious. I thought that I was trying to solve my problems by worrying or rushing into decisions I didn't need to make. In reality I was probably not helping much at all, and in some cases I was making my problems worse.

Trusting God sounds like it should be the easiest thing in the world to do, but it wasn't something that came naturally to me. If anyone asked, I always would say that I trusted God, but that wasn't how I behaved. I never associated worrying with not trusting God. In fact, I didn't give much thought to worrying at all, because I didn't see it as something I could control. I'd become so used to worrying that it felt like part of my personality—it was who I was, a worrier. When I think back, even praying about my troubles wasn't so much handing them over and trusting God as another opportunity to go over and over any problems in my mind.

I watched friends who I knew had issues that would cause many people worry, yet they still seemed to have fun and enjoy themselves. I wasn't sure that I could be so joyful in similar situations. Looking back, I realise that I missed chances to enjoy some wonderful experiences by having my mind caught up in speculation and over-analysis. I'd be worried about something that might or might not happen in the future, or else be tied up with thoughts of a past I could not change. I wasn't alone in this way of thinking. According to a YouGov survey of 2300 adults in Britain, carried out for Mental Health Awareness week 2014, almost one in five people feel anxious all of the time or a lot of the time (*Living with Anxiety: Understanding the role and impact of anxiety in our lives*, Mental Health Awareness Week 2014, Mental Health Foundation). Of course, it's only natural to feel worried when faced with life-changing situations, but many of us are living at that constantly heightened level of anxiety all the time.

When worry becomes our normal way of thinking, it is difficult to take on Jesus' advice to live one day at a time and trust God that our needs will be met. Yet, I think Jesus knows that it's not easy. If it was, he would have had no need to preach about it. He knows that it is something we have to do consciously and that it takes effort. But how much energy and effort does it take to worry? Worry is tiring, isn't it? Wouldn't it be so much easier if we could hand all those energy-zapping thoughts to God and get on with enjoying our lives?

Sometimes we learn to lean on God by practising letting go of small everyday anxieties. Other times it takes a situation so clearly out of our control that we have nowhere else to turn but God before we truly experience what it means to put our trust in him. Whatever situation you find yourself in, there are opportunities to lean on God every day and let him support you. Today we are going to use those opportunities, however small, to practise letting go of our worries and trusting God to meet our needs.

It took me a long time to learn really to let go and trust God, but when I did, I found it very freeing. I enjoy my life a lot more. I am more present in the moment, and by letting go of a control I'd falsely assumed, I also feel less vulnerable. I don't need to keep thinking about the same problem over and over, because I know that if there is something I can do to help my situation, then God will guide me. In this way I am more open to and can better recognise opportunities that could help solve my problems; chances I might have overlooked when my thoughts were consumed with worry.

Of course, this change in my outlook didn't happen overnight and it is something I'm still practising. Sometimes I think I've given a problem to God, and then I find myself worrying about it and realise I've taken my problem back and need to hand it over again. When I'm finding it more difficult to let go and trust God with a particular problem, I find it helpful to use something physical to signify handing the issue over. In my garden I have smooth pebbles on the tops of my plant pots. They look pretty and also help protect the plants from losing too much water in the summer months. When I begin to worry about something, I hold one of the pebbles in my hand and pray about the situation. Then I put the pebble down and whenever I find the problem coming up in my mind, I can look out on to the garden and know it is OK, because I've given it to God. Although I might not understand or like my situation, I remind myself that God is in control, that he will sustain me and work all things out for good.

TODAY'S PRACTICE

1 Find 15 minutes in your day to sit quietly, close your eyes, take in a couple of deep breaths to help you relax, and be still in the presence of God. Imagine you are breathing in God's love and breathing out anything that is troubling you.

2 Today, practise letting go of your worries quickly and trusting God. If, like me, you find it helpful to do something physical to hand over your worry, find a way that signifies this for you. I like using pebbles because I can hold them in my hand while I'm praying, and laying them on the ground feels like I've let go of a weight. If you don't have a garden, you can do the same with a houseplant, or a bowl of decorative pebbles on a table or windowsill. Alternatively, you might find it helpful to write down any worries in a private notebook, or on a piece of paper that you fold up and place in a tin or a box. If you find your thoughts coming back to whatever was worrying you, look at the plant, bowl, notebook, box, or whatever you find easiest to use, and know that you've given to God whatever is in there. You don't need to worry about it any longer because he has got everything under control.

3 At the end of the day, spend five minutes thinking about any good things that have happened and things that you have

enjoyed. Fill the space for today's diary entry. Don't stop writing until the space is full. It doesn't matter how big or small the thing is that you choose to write down. All that matters is that you are noting something good that happened today. When you have written your list, thank God for all the things that are on it.

DAY 21

REFLECT ON YOUR WEEK

Then Peter came to Jesus and asked, 'Lord, how many times shall I forgive my brother or sister who sins against me? Up to seven times?' Jesus answered, 'I tell you, not seven times, but seventy times seven.'

MATTHEW 18:21–22

Letting go of hurts, regrets and unmet expectations in life is never easy. As Jesus clearly tells us, it is also not something that we do once and then that's the end of it. Sometimes we will find ourselves needing to let go of the same issues over and over again. We can think that we have let a hurt go, but then we are reminded of a painful situation, or a person who has hurt us deeply in the past does something else to upset us. If we try to explain this to others, this recent incident may seem like a small thing to them. But we are not hurting from that one thing; we are reeling from all the other pains that have gone before, pains that we thought we'd dealt with until they come back just as acutely. It is only human to feel this way. In time, as we practice letting go of hurts quickly, we find that although we may feel the same physical pang, we are able to let go of the hurt and begin healing more easily and quicker than before. Forgiveness and letting go cuts our ties to a painful past and gives us the freedom to make the most of our future. In order to enjoy that future, we need to keep moving forward and stay open to love in all its forms and wherever it appears. Trust God to heal you and believe fully in your heart that he works all things out for the good of all concerned.

Looking back over the exercises in the week, were there any that you found more challenging than others? Why do you think that was? Are there any experiences that surprised you? Did any issues arise that you would consider significant? Are there any changes that you would like to make as a result of your experiences this week?

TODAY'S PRACTICE

1 Find 15 minutes in your day to sit quietly, close your eyes, take in a couple of deep breaths to help you relax, and be still in the presence of God. Imagine you are breathing in God's love and breathing out anything that is troubling you.

2 At the end of the day, spend five minutes thinking about any good things that have happened and things that you have enjoyed. Fill the space for today's diary entry. Don't stop writing until the space is full. It doesn't matter how big or small the thing is that you choose to write down. All that matters is that you are noting something good that happened today. When you have written your list, thank God for all the things that are on it.

WEEK 4

REACH OUT

What good is it, my brothers and sisters, if someone claims to have faith but has no deeds? Can such faith save them?

JAMES 2:14

DAY 22

SHARE YOUR GIFTS

Each of you should use whatever gift you have received to serve others, as faithful stewards of God's grace in its various forms.

1 PETER 4:10

It is often said that if we all did our part, then the world would be a better place. But what is our part? We all want to feel that what we do matters, that our being in the world makes a difference, and that we are needed in some way. How we do this is a question for which each individual receives a unique answer, and that answer can and frequently does change depending on when the question is asked.

Over the years I've met many people who complain of leading hollow, empty lives devoid of purpose. These people desperately want their lives to feel more meaningful yet don't know how to change their situation or even where to start. For them, it seems that there are two kinds of people: those who are very clear about their role in the world, and others, like them, who are forever searching for a meaning that they never quite grasp. A large part of this struggle seems to come from trying to find one thing that they are meant to do—a single pursuit, career, achievement or relationship that they could point to as their reason for living. In focusing on finding that one thing, many people take their natural strengths for granted and stop valuing them.

I think lots of us have been there at one time. I know I

have. It is why the 1946 film *It's a Wonderful Life* (directed by Frank Capra) resonates strongly with so many people. It tells the story of George Bailey, played by James Stewart, who contemplates suicide because he believes that he has achieved nothing in his life and that everyone would be better off if he had never been born. Facing despair, George is encouraged by a guardian angel called Clarence (Henry Travers) who shows him what life in the small town of Bedford Falls would have been like without him. Seeing life from a different perspective helps George to appreciate the positive part he has played in the lives of so many people in the town, and in the heart of the town itself. Instead of thinking about his life as humdrum and worthless, he suddenly recognises its significance and realises that far from being worthless, it is indeed wonderful.

We won't all be a prime minister, a famous actor, a celebrated musician, a CEO of a multi-national company, a dot.com billionaire, a parent, a grandparent, a modern-day superhero, or whatever you have been holding up as your definition of having 'made something' of your life; but we can all live with love, make the most of our natural strengths, and encourage others to do the same.

The person who taught me this more than any other was a man called Bill Griffiths (whose story is told in greater length in the book *Against the Odds*, BRF, 2014). If you are tempted to think that you have no useful talents or skills, bear in mind that simply by holding this book and reading the words on the page you are doing two things that Bill was unable to do for most of his adult life. At the age of 21, Bill was conscripted to fight in World War II. He left behind his family haulage business, his wife and his newborn child to travel halfway across the world to Singapore. His regiment had set out to rescue 200 stranded Royal Air Force men and ended up being herded into lorries as Far Eastern Prisoners of War under Japanese rule. When the lorry doors opened, Bill was thrown on to a roadside and faced with more than 20 Japanese guards pointing their bayonets in his direction. He was ordered to remove netting from an ammunitions dump. Knowing it to be dangerous, he tugged the netting gently, but the movement was enough to set off a live grenade.

When Bill regained consciousness, he awoke to find his leg in plaster from foot to hip, his hands gone, and he had lost his sight. For a while he fell into despair, feeling that he was useless, and that his life was not worth living any more. Once his leg healed, Bill was able to leave his bed and talk to other men in the hospital. By sharing stories he soon realised that, blind or sighted, whole or maimed, all the prisoners were hungry, frightened and weary, and it was the job of each one of them to keep spirits up in the camp. From that day on, as far as he could, Bill put on an air of cheerfulness, whistling and singing wherever he went. That way, he felt he might have a part to play in helping others, and it gave his life purpose again.

After another three-and-a-half years, the war ended, Bill was liberated and he went on to lead a long life that was fuller and richer than he ever could have imagined in the immediate aftermath of his injuries. He always focused on what he could do, and how he could use his talents and abilities to help others, and in so doing achieved successes that most people would have deemed impossible.

For each of us, the path we envision for our life gives it meaning. Our setbacks may not be as traumatic or disabling as Bill's, but if our path is diverted we can find ourselves at a loss as to who we are or what our purpose is. Yet, as Bill shows, our purpose in life isn't fixed. What we are able to do, what we enjoy doing and what we excel at will change over time. Our purpose comes from recognising what we can do to help others, right here, right now, and knowing that by taking action in this way, we have done our part.

TODAY'S PRACTICE

1 Find 15 minutes in your day to sit quietly, close your eyes, take in a couple of deep breaths to help you relax, and be still in the presence of God. Imagine you are breathing in God's love and breathing out anything that is troubling you.

2 Take time to recognise and appreciate your natural strengths by focusing on what you can do in any particular situation. Look for a way that you can use your talents, skills or abilities to be of help to someone today. Notice and resist any times when you restrict yourself by thinking things like: it's not my job to do that, or it's not my turn, or someone else could do it. Whatever help you give, do it generously and with a sincere heart, knowing that your purpose can be many things at many times. You will not always know the wider impact of your actions, or how God is using you for good. If more than one opportunity comes up to help someone, go for it!

3 At the end of the day, spend five minutes thinking about any good things that have happened and things that you have enjoyed. Fill the space for today's diary entry. Don't stop writing until the space is full. It doesn't matter how big or small the thing is that you choose to write down. All that matters is that you are noting something good that happened today. When you have written your list, thank God for all the things that are on it.

DAY 23

ASK FOR HELP

So I say to you: ask and it will be given to you; seek and you will find; knock and the door will be opened to you.

LUKE 11:9

It's a strange fact that while a large part of growing up is about learning to be independent, one of life's greatest lessons is realising that you don't need to do everything on your own. Unfortunately, some people don't ask for what they need because they believe that doing so would be a sign of weakness. Other people may fear being turned down and the rejection, hurt or embarrassment they might feel as a result. It takes strength to ask for help, particularly after a difficult experience. It reveals a hope for something better. By asking for help, we are saying that we want and believe our life can improve. We are letting people know that we value ourselves. At the same time, we are expressing that we value other people and appreciate the part they can play in making our lives better.

Until we ask, we may never know who could help us, what form that help might take, and how others too might benefit from our request. When 67-year-old Alan Barnes was attacked outside his home in Gateshead, Tyne and Wear, he could never have imagined how far his cries for help would be heard. It was six o'clock on a Sunday evening and he was putting his bin out for collection when a young man knocked him to the ground and demanded money. Alan said honestly that he didn't have any money, but as he lay on the ground the man continued to rifle through his pockets, eventually fleeing the scene empty-handed. Although he didn't know it at the time, Alan had broken his collarbone in the fall, but he managed to get to his feet and alert a neighbour about what had happened. The neighbour then telephoned Alan's sister, Carol, who took him to the hospital and then back to her home because he was too afraid to return to his council flat, where until this time he had happily lived independently and alone.

Alan reported what had happened to the police, who informed the media in a bid to help find his attacker. The story made headlines because it was such a cowardly and cruel attack. Alan was born with a number of disabilities, including growth problems, and is registered blind. At a height of 4ft 6inches and weighing less than six stones, it was clear for anyone to see that he couldn't have put up any kind of a fight. The newspaper reports expressed outrage that anyone could attack such a vulnerable member of society. No doubt most people who read the story shared this view, but just 20 minutes away from where he lived, Katie Cutler, a 21-year-old woman he'd never met, was putting her young daughter to bed when she heard Alan's story on the news. Katie was so moved that she wanted to do something to show Alan he was cared for. Perhaps if she could raise a bit of money, when Alan found somewhere else to live he could buy new carpets and curtains to make it feel homely.

To help her raise some money, Katie set up a page on GoFundMe.com with a target of £500, briefly explaining what had happened to Alan. 'We can't take away what has happened,' she wrote, 'but with a little donation we can make the future a prettier one and help towards the cost of his new home.' Less than an hour later Katie's fundraising target had been met, and the donations kept on coming. When Katie closed the fund 24 days later, almost 25,000 people from all over the world had donated to the cause, raising more than £330,000, with many more people and businesses offering their services to help Alan settle into his new home.

Alan was overwhelmed by the response. Katie's gesture had reminded him of what he always knew—that there are far more good people in the world than bad. Even before his broken bones had healed, Alan knew that he would remember people's generosity and love more than anything else about his ordeal.

The money raised was enough to buy Alan a new home, and for him to start some charity work of his own, helping young people in his church. Katie didn't gain anything for herself in financial terms, but in reaching out she too made a new friend in Alan, and she said that her heart had been warmed from the lifetime of compliments she had received within a few days.

When given the opportunity, most people enjoy helping others, whether through sharing knowledge, time, skills or money. There are some who, for whatever reason, cannot or will not help us. When that happens, often we make it into a much bigger deal that it needs to be. OK, our pride may be a bit bruised and we may feel disappointed and disheartened, but aside from that, we're not in a worse situation than we were before we asked. We didn't have what we wanted before we requested help, and we don't have it now. Rather than worrying why or getting upset, pray about it and look to the next person who might be the one to help you make the change. If we can find the courage to do so, life would often be a lot easier—we would give people an opportunity to show us they care; we would heal faster; we would achieve more than we ever could do alone; and, like Alan and Katie, we may end up with much more than we could have ever dreamed of asking for.

TODAY'S PRACTICE

1 Find 15 minutes in your day to sit quietly, close your eyes, take in a couple of deep breaths to help you relax, and be still in the presence of God. Imagine you are breathing in God's love and breathing out anything that is troubling you.

2 Today, take any opportunities to ask for support, help or guidance from God in prayer, and from the people around you. When communicating with those closest to you, don't assume that they should know what you want, and similarly don't assume that you know what they want either—ask. If you are the kind of person who always helps others but rarely accepts any help in return, it may be difficult to take up any opportunities to ask for help. Start with a small request like asking someone to recommend a restaurant or a film. Gradually move on to a request that you may find more difficult to make, because receiving it would mean a lot to you. If you are knocked back, remind yourself that you are no worse off than you were before you asked. Everyone has been turned down for something at some time in life. Don't let a setback put you off asking again. In time, if your request is for the good of all concerned, God will guide the right person to your path who will say yes.

3 At the end of the day, spend five minutes thinking about any good things that have happened and things that you have

enjoyed. Fill the space for today's diary entry. Don't stop writing until the space is full. It doesn't matter how big or small the thing is that you choose to write down. All that matters is that you are noting something good that happened today. When you have written your list, thank God for all the things that are on it.

DAY 24

RECOGNISE KINDNESS
AND BE KIND

Keep on loving one another as brothers and sisters. Do not
forget to show hospitality to strangers, for by so doing some
people have shown hospitality to angels without knowing it.
HEBREWS 13:1–2

The summer of 2011 in the UK will be remembered for
violence, looting and arson as rioting spread across numerous
towns and cities in what was the biggest display of civil unrest
for decades. It's easy to feel hopeless and helpless when faced
with a situation like that. What can one person do to make
a difference? Is it possible to change the world just by being
kind?

That was the question raised in a thought-provoking
theatre show I reviewed called *366 Days of Kindness*, by
London-based actress and comedienne Bernadette Russell,[10]
during which I was picked out of the audience and handed
a piece of paper with 'A COMPLIMENT', written in extra
large letters on one side, and a drawing of a woman with
curly hair, like mine, on the other with the words, 'You have
the greatest hair.' In this quirky aside, Bernadette got me to
experience her message as well as hear it. By that one small
act of kindness I would remember her.

As Bernadette readily admits, her show isn't based on an
original premise, but it made me smile, and, in my view, the
world can never have too much kindness.

Indeed, there didn't appear to be much kindness around at all when Bernadette began her 'good deed crusade', in which she surprised a stranger with an act of kindness every day for a year. I say 'crusade' because at times she forced her kind acts on people, whether they were welcomed or not—which, as she now recognises, is not very kind. This in-your-face kindness was Bernadette's response to the in-your-face violence of the 2011 riots, in which family businesses were torched and a student was robbed as he lay bleeding in the street.

During her leap year of kindness, Bernadette bought flowers for strangers, dressed phone boxes as magic boxes, handed out sweets, gave away books and sent numerous well-wishing cards. She once opened her loo to the public during the London Marathon, but in hindsight reveals that wasn't her best idea.

The outcome is a personal journey as much as a comment on society. To many people, Bernadette's appearance is that of a brash comedienne who wears bright red lipstick in the daytime and does crazy things without thinking. As a child she ate a goldfish, gave her sister pee to drink, and kicked a boy because he looked like Simon Le Bon! Her immediate response to violence was an angry, forceful kindness, but by the end of the year of good deeds it moved into something softer. Could this be because kindness has a positive effect, not just on the person at the receiving end, but on the person who is showing kindness too?

Many scientific studies have shown that acting kindly has both physical and mental health benefits, by reducing stress, boosting the immune system, and increasing happiness and overall satisfaction in life.[11] Practising random acts of kindness, as Bernadette does, may seem gimmicky to some, but it is a good way to experience the joy of giving without expecting anything in return.

Thinking more consciously about ways in which we can show kindness can open us up to recognising just how many acts of kindness we experience ourselves, every day. It is easy to take small kindnesses and courtesies for granted. Yet, as we learned from Ray Rossiter's story on Day 15, when all dignity and comfort are stripped away, small acts of kindness and compassion become magnified and can play a large part in helping people to survive. During World War II, Ray was captured by the Japanese in Singapore and held as a prisoner of war for three-and-a-half years. Thirty years after he was liberated, Ray attended an event organised by the National Federation of Far Eastern Prisoners of War, of which he had once been President. As he entered the room, a man approached him sincerely and said, 'Thank you for that drink of water.' At first Ray didn't recognise the man or know what he was talking about, but as the man started to explain, he remembered clearly.

During their time as prisoners, Ray had found this man at the side of a jungle track where he'd fallen with exhaustion. Ray was carrying a bottle made out of coconut shell. He had only a mouthful of water left in it, but it was enough to revive the man so that he could continue walking, and they carried on the trail together. Ray said that it was nothing to him, just a drop of water from his bottle, but it was everything to the other man, and he never forgot it.

Our act of kindness may seem small to us, but we don't know how God may be using it to influence positively the life of someone else. When, in the Bible, Abraham is sent messengers from God, they appear to him in the form of men, with whom he shares his food and drink, extending his hospitality by providing water to wash and a place to rest (Genesis 18). For thousands of years God has spoken to us through our interactions with other people. Sometimes the timing of our meeting or the nature of help we receive will lead us to describe these people as angels. Whether these strangers to us are heavenly messengers or simply coincidental companions on life's journey, we are all one body in Christ, and treating others well benefits everyone (Romans 12:5).

TODAY'S PRACTICE

1 Find 15 minutes in your day to sit quietly, close your eyes, take in a couple of deep breaths to help you relax, and be still in the presence of God. Imagine you are breathing in God's love and breathing out anything that is troubling you.

2 Look out for and record any kindness you experience, witness, read or hear about today. Notice and appreciate any kindness you had perhaps been taking for granted, such as family helping around the house; a colleague making a cup of tea; a friend listening to your news, or the stranger who holds a door open. Use your list to think about ways in which you can be kinder, and take up any opportunities to be kind.

3 At the end of the day, spend five minutes thinking about any good things that have happened and things that you have enjoyed. Fill the space for today's diary entry. Don't stop writing until the space is full. It doesn't matter how big or small the thing is that you choose to write down. All that matters is that you are noting something good that happened today. When you have written your list, thank God for all the things that are on it.

DAY 25

CONNECT WITH THOSE AROUND YOU

Two are better than one, because they have a good return
for their labour: if either of them falls down, one can help
the other up.

ECCLESIASTES 4:9–10

When you live in a large city, as I do, it can be easy to think of
people as simply another part of the landscape. The more of
them there are, the more each face blurs into the next. Some
people enjoy this anonymity, the ability to slip into a crowd
and become unknown and unnoticed. For other people, the
same situation can feel very lonely—being surrounded by
people but not recognising any as human beings who they
can reach out to, even in conversation.

I had this experience recently when I was travelling on a
busy London bus. I knew that I'd got on the right bus service
for where I wanted to go, but having never been to that part
of the city before, I wouldn't recognise when I had got there
and therefore at which stop to get off. Not wanting to bother
the driver, I hoped the woman who stood closest to me might
be able to help. 'Excuse me?' I said gently, hoping she would
look in my direction so that I could ask her. The woman
averted her eyes deliberately, like a child playing the game
of covering her face and thinking that because she can't see
me anymore, I can't see her either. I decided to ask someone
else but she ignored me as well, this time turning her whole

body so that she was facing away from me. It was clear that simply by trying to speak, I had become the nutter on the bus who must be avoided at all costs. Realising this, I sighed and said more loudly, 'Oh, for goodness' sake, I'm only trying to ask where I need to get off the bus.' A voice from the back asked me where I wanted to be. After I replied, several people rushed to answer me. Suddenly the whole bus was alive with conversation. It felt like the passengers had been given permission to speak safely. I only wanted directions; everything was OK.

That situation on the bus was extreme, but it made me think about how many different ways we shut people out of our lives, or pretend that we don't see them, for fear of what they might want from us—and not just strangers on the street, but extended family members, friends and colleagues.

When we're not alone ourselves, it can be difficult to understand how others might at times feel isolated and lonely. We put off visiting an elderly relative because we haven't got time; we don't call on a sick neighbour in case they ask us to do something and begin to rely on us for help; or we don't answer a friend's phone call because we assume she'll want to chat for an hour and it's easier not to pick up than to say a quick 'hello' and ask when would be a good time to call back. Because we are worried about that part of ourselves we can't give, we sometimes choose to give nothing at all.

Mother Teresa once told a story about a man she met while walking through the streets of London. He was sitting doubled up and looking so lonely. Noticing this, Mother Teresa went over to him. She shook his hand and asked simply, 'How are you?' The man sat up, his eyes now full of joy and said, 'After a long, long time I feel the warmth of a human hand.' Mother Teresa told how that man was a different being, just because there was a human hand that made him feel that yes he was somebody, somebody who was loved.

If I'm honest, I would often prefer the shops to be quieter, the streets to be less crowded, and for there to be less traffic on the roads. I could get more done, in less time, with a lot less hassle. On the flip side, fewer people probably couldn't sustain the number of facilities on my doorstep that I enjoy. I sometimes remind myself of this when I'm busy scanning my surroundings for where people are not: the spare seat on public transport, the shorter queue in the supermarket, the empty table in a café. I remind myself that within these crowds are people who feel lonely. A smile, a kind word or polite courtesy may be all they need to feel that they are not alone and that, if they fall down, there is someone to help them up.

TODAY'S PRACTICE

1 Find 15 minutes in your day to sit quietly, close your eyes, take in a couple of deep breaths to help you relax, and be still in the presence of God. Imagine you are breathing in God's love and breathing out anything that is troubling you.

2 Is there someone you've been meaning to get in contact with but you have been putting it off because you felt you haven't had the time? If there is, take time today to visit, write a card, send an email or make a phone call—whatever you can do to get in touch. As you go through your day, you may cross paths with many people, some you will know and some you don't. Introduce yourself to the new person in your workplace;

welcome the new visitor to church; and if you are in a job where you work with the public, be friendly and helpful to those who use your service, because you don't know if yours might be the only smile they see today.

3 At the end of the day, spend five minutes thinking about any good things that have happened and things that you have enjoyed. Fill the space for today's diary entry. Don't stop writing until the space is full. It doesn't matter how big or small the thing is that you choose to write down. All that matters is that you are noting something good that happened today. When you have written your list, thank God for all the things that are on it.

BE GENEROUS WITH YOUR TIME

And let us consider how we may spur one another on toward love and good deeds, not giving up meeting together, as some are in the habit of doing, but encouraging one another.

HEBREWS 10:24–25

When I was growing up we had a dog called Prince. My parents had never planned to get a dog. Indeed, despite my constant pleas, they were adamant not to have one. Then my granddad's dog Bess escaped from the garden one day and before long there was a litter of pups in his house. 'I saved one for you,' he told me on the phone one day.

'I'm not having a dog. Who is going to look after it?' said my mum.

'I'll look after him,' I said, not knowing at six years old what looking after anything involved. My mum raised her eyebrows in a knowing look. 'I will,' I insisted.

'So, you'll walk him, every day, whatever the weather?' my dad asked.

'Yes, I will. I'll look after him, I promise,' I said.

'Well, you're saying that now, but what if you get fed up of him? Who is going to look after him then?' my mum asked.

'Why would I get fed up of him?'

Knowing full well that there is no use arguing with a child, my parents decided to leave it there, hoping I'd forget about it. My granddad lived three hours' drive away. When we visited in the next school holidays, the pup would no doubt have a new home, and my head would have been turned by something else entirely.

As that time approached all the pups had gone to good homes—all except Prince. Thinking practically about a pet that would take up less time, my parents had decided we could get a cat instead. We then found out that my brother is allergic to cats, which put an end to that idea. It seemed that everything was lining up in my favour. How could my parents say 'no' now?

They didn't. Once we saw Prince, the whole family fell in love, albeit some more reluctantly than others. I couldn't be happier.

Until the day I went to university I did as I'd promised every day: I walked Prince and my dad came with us. It never felt like a chore because I enjoyed being with Prince, and I enjoyed spending time talking to my dad without any distractions of household chores or work or phones or other people or TV. I still enjoy spending time with and talking to my dad. We are great friends, but that's not simply because he's my dad. It's because he has always taken time, and still does, to listen to me and be interested in what is happening in my life.

Looking back on those years we had Prince I realise how lucky I was, not simply to get my wish for a dog, but to get to spend such quality time with my dad. Today it is thought that on average families spend little more than half-an-hour of quality time together on a weekday, and less than eight hours over a full week. There are lots of reasons for this, including long and anti-social working hours, household chores, TV, computer games and evening clubs. I'm not saying that everyone should go and get a dog, but I do think that just as we had to commit to looking after Prince, everyone in a family needs to commit to spending quality time together as a routine.

Of all the people we love, it is easiest in some ways to overlook making time for those closest to us, and to fail to show an interest in their lives and wellbeing. Of course, if asked, we would say that spending time with these people is the most important thing in the world to us, but when we see people every day it's easy to fall into the trap of thinking that we don't need to set aside any quality time with them. We need to be able to relax at home, but that isn't the same as spending all our energy elsewhere so that our family gets to spend time only with our exhausted self.

You can't give generously of your time to everyone, but your time is a gift that you give to someone each day, even if that someone is yourself. We all have increasing demands on our time, but unless we make relationships a priority for us, there will always be something else demanding our attention. At first it may seem an effort to find space to spend quality time with loved ones, but in the strongest relationships spending quality time together becomes a routine. In the end, it is our routines that shape our lives. Yes, our time is precious, but in giving generously of our time we cannot lose, because in accepting our gift, the other person is giving us the gift of their time right back.

TODAY'S PRACTICE

1   Find 15 minutes in your day to sit quietly, close your eyes, take in a couple of deep breaths to help you relax, and be still in the

presence of God. Imagine you are breathing in God's love and breathing out anything that is troubling you.

2 Think about the people in your life: family, friends, work colleagues and neighbours. Who needs your undivided attention today? Think about something that person might like to do, extend an invitation and tell them it's on you. It doesn't have to be extravagant. It could be an afternoon stroll in the park, going to a coffee shop, or cooking a meal for them. If the person is someone within your home, your response could be as simple as asking about your spouse's day, helping your daughter with her homework, taking your son to a sport game, or not answering your mobile phone during a family meal. If no one immediately comes to mind, pray and ask God, 'Who in my life needs my undivided attention right now?' You might be surprised at the person God places in your heart.

3 At the end of the day, spend five minutes thinking about any good things that have happened and things that you have enjoyed. Fill the space for today's diary entry. Don't stop writing until the space is full. It doesn't matter how big or small the thing is that you choose to write down. All that matters is that you are noting something good that happened today. When you have written your list, thank God for all the things that are on it.

DAY 27

GIVE AND TAKE

Each of you should give what you have decided in your heart to give, not reluctantly or under compulsion, for God loves a cheerful giver.

2 CORINTHIANS 9:7

When I was at university I shared a large house with twelve other students. Inside the door there was a huge porch with bench seating on either side, and every evening we opened it up for homeless people to come and sit inside. We all took it in turns on different days to pour cups of sugary tea and make sandwiches, and after a while we got to recognise a small group of regulars who we knew by name.

It was a routine we got into, although some of my housemates clearly enjoyed helping out more than others. For Stephan, I could see that it was a real joy to be able to give in this way. He didn't need to be on a rota because he helped out most days and would spend hours talking to people over several cups of tea.

One of our regular visitors was an older man called Bob, and Stephan would sometimes invite him inside to use the bath. Although I could see it was a generous thing to do, it made me feel uncomfortable because the bathroom Bob used was opposite my bedroom. He never locked the door, and on more than one occasion I opened the door, unaware that anyone was bathing in there.

It was difficult to explain to Stephan how this made me

feel without sounding uncharitable, so, after my initial surprise at finding Bob in the bath, I didn't say anything. I couldn't say I was happy about it, but for me it wasn't worth arguing about. Over time, however, there were other things that did start to bother me, like when I opened the fridge one evening to cook and my food had gone. I thought perhaps another member of the household had mistaken it for theirs and eaten it, but Stephan admitted that a stranger had come to the door and was hungry so he'd given it away.

'But it wasn't your food to give, Stephan,' I told him.

Stephan apologised, but he didn't offer to replace my food. Now, I was hungry. There were no shops open nearby and I didn't have much spare cash in any case. Perhaps I should have felt pleased that my dinner had gone to feed someone who really needed it, but I didn't. Nor did I feel happy when someone let a drunken man into the porch and left him unattended so that he got into the house, where he shouted and chased me with a knife. I made it safely to my room and locked the door, but I didn't have a mobile phone so I stayed there until morning, because I was too afraid to come out. So you won't be surprised to hear that I wasn't overjoyed when, during the summer, we let a homeless woman move in with us.

I still remember the conversation we had around the dinner table, because I was the one who was most vocal in arguing against the idea.

'I think it's awful too that she has nowhere to live,' I said, 'but this is my home, and now I don't feel safe.'

'We're Christians. We have to let her sleep here if we have room,' was the response.

Reluctantly I agreed she could stay, but I remember thinking that perhaps I wasn't really a Christian after all, because a real Christian would have been happy to help in this way.

For the next couple of weeks I rang round various churches, looking for someone who would help me find the woman some accommodation, but I didn't succeed. I don't know what happened to her or if she ever found a more stable place to live. One day, after a few weeks, we woke up and she had gone. In the autumn I moved out too.

For a while I stopped going to church because I felt that I wasn't good enough. I wasn't long past my teenage years, and, like many teenagers, I'd turned my experience into a melodrama. In reality, I'd simply been in a situation where I was giving, reluctantly, what wasn't in my heart to give at that time. My being miserable wasn't helping anyone. I was giving, but it was under pressure, and once that pressure was off I wasn't going to continue doing it. Instead, I needed to find something that gave me the same joy from giving that Stephan found by opening our house to strangers in need, but something more suited to my skills and personality.

Over the years since then, I have given time and money to help many different causes, and I can honestly say that when I give cheerfully it doesn't feel as if I am giving at all, because what I get in return is so much more. It was only when I found a way to enjoy giving that I understood Jesus' words, 'It is more blessed to give than to receive' (Acts 20:35). Through volunteering both formally and informally, I've made new friends with common interests, strengthened existing friendships and done things that have given me a sense of purpose and contribution.

I'm not alone in feeling this way. Research has shown that volunteering is beneficial for those who help as well as those who are helped. It has a positive impact on both physical and mental health, and helps people to develop solid support systems by keeping them in regular contact with others.[12]

Everyone needs to feel a sense of belonging and value. If you can find a job where your heart is, you're very fortunate, but if it's just to pay the groceries at the end of the week, volunteering can give you that sense of contribution. There are so many ways to volunteer today: whatever you're interested in, you'll find some encouragement if you're willing to give some time. The most important requirement is that, whatever you choose to give, you do it gladly with a compassionate heart.

We can all benefit from a more caring society, but community doesn't just happen; it is something we need to work together to achieve. Here lies the challenge, because it requires more than money: it demands a change of heart. Whatever some people might say, volunteering is not about giving something for nothing. If you don't receive anything, then very soon you'll stop giving anything. You have to get something out of it yourself.

By volunteering, in whatever way, we're helping and supporting each other, and that's how life should be. God loves a cheerful giver, because it is by giving cheerfully that we begin to understand and experience the joy of God's love.

TODAY'S PRACTICE

1 Find 15 minutes in your day to sit quietly, close your eyes, take in a couple of deep breaths to help you relax, and be still in the presence of God. Imagine you are breathing in God's love and breathing out anything that is troubling you.

2 Think about a cause that is close to your heart, or an area of life

in which you would like to make a difference. How much time can you reasonably commit—an hour a week, or longer? Think about what you are good at and what you enjoy. Perhaps if you work in an office all day you might like to do something outdoors, like helping with a community allotment or an outdoor sports club. If you would like a dog but don't have the time for one of your own, you can be put in touch with people who need help walking their pets. Whatever you decide, it doesn't have to be a big commitment. Even something like offering to bring in the bins for a frail neighbour, taking a turn to lead the walking school bus or joining your local neighbourhood watch scheme can improve life for people around you while helping you to feel a stronger part of the community. If the cause that comes to mind is one where you feel you can't do something directly, you might make a regular donation to a charity that can. You could sponsor a child to enable them to continue schooling overseas, write letters of encouragement to someone in prison, sign a government petition, or start a petition of your own. If you are a regular volunteer already, think about what aspects of volunteering you most enjoy, and recognise the benefits it brings to your life as well as to others.

3 At the end of the day, spend five minutes thinking about any good things that have happened and things that you have enjoyed. Fill the space for today's diary entry. Don't stop writing until the space is full. It doesn't matter how big or small the thing is that you choose to write down. All that matters is that you are noting something good that happened today. When you have written your list, thank God for all the things that are on it.

DAY 28

REFLECT ON YOUR WEEK

'Give, and it will be given to you. A good measure, pressed
down, shaken together and running over, will be poured
into your lap. For with the measure you use, it will be
measured to you.'

LUKE 6:38

Someone once said, 'We make a living by what we get,
but we make a life by what we give.' When I look at my
own life, this is true. The areas where I give most reflect
my personality, because I choose to use my time, money
and skills in the parts of my life that are most important to
me—but it hasn't always been the case. Sometimes when
we get hurt we can withdraw from other people. After all,
if we don't allow ourselves to get close, then we can't get
rejected. The problem with this logic is that it leads us to feel
more isolated. I hope that some of the exercises this week
have helped you to gain confidence in reaching out to other
people and in using your unique set of skills and talents to
help others.

It is easy to become distracted by other people and to be
pushed in a particular direction. We can give reluctantly,
until we become miserable, and then wonder why we have
no energy left to give in other areas of our lives. We all have
something we can contribute; our purpose comes from
recognising what God has placed on our heart to do, and

stepping out in confidence to do it. Remember that being able to give is a gift in itself.

Looking back over the exercises in the week, were there any that you found more challenging than others? Why do you think that was? Did any experiences surprise you? Did any issues arise that you would consider significant? Are there any changes that you would like to make as a result of your experiences this week?

TODAY'S PRACTICE

1 Find 15 minutes in your day to sit quietly, close your eyes, take in a couple of deep breaths to help you relax, and be still in the presence of God. Imagine you are breathing in God's love and breathing out anything that is troubling you.

2 At the end of the day, spend five minutes thinking about any good things that have happened and things that you have enjoyed. Fill the space for today's diary entry. Don't stop writing until the space is full. It doesn't matter how big or small the thing is that you choose to write down. All that matters is that you are noting something good that happened today. When you have written your list, thank God for all the things that are on it.

WEEK 5

LOVE YOUR LIFE

Take delight in the Lord, and he will give you
the desires of your heart.

PSALM 37:4

SAY THANK YOU

Praise the Lord, my soul, and forget not all his benefits.
PSALM 103:2

During the last four weeks you have been recording some of the good things in your life. If you weren't consciously writing them down every day, do you think you would have noticed the number of blessings you've received in this time? When I first started keeping my list, I was surprised at how much good God was doing in my life. I was going through a difficult time and felt that I didn't have much to celebrate at all. I had become so wrapped up in my problems that I was unable to see anything else. In reality, there was a lot of good in my life, and my list was only scratching the surface of all I had to be thankful for.

Wherever you are in your life right now, in reading this book you can do what 775 million adults who are illiterate cannot do. If you're in a room, you may have a light switched on, or music or a TV playing. If so, you are enjoying something that a quarter of the world's population cannot, because they don't have access to electricity. Have you turned a tap on today? Did you give it a second thought? There are 783 million people in the world (about eleven per cent of the population) who do not have access to safe water. Have you used the bathroom? Across the globe there are 2.5 billion people who do not have access to adequate sanitation, and in sub-Saharan Africa only 31 per cent of people are able to access a toilet. Have you eaten today? I'm not talking about a gourmet meal—I mean, have you eaten anything at all? Tonight, one in seven people in the world will go to bed hungry, and by the end of the day almost 16,000 children will have died from hunger-related causes. That's one child every five seconds. Even with all the technological and medical advances of recent decades, hunger still kills more people than any disease—more than AIDS, malaria and tuberculosis combined.

Statistics like these can be difficult to comprehend. I don't use them to belittle any problems you may be going through, but to help you recognise some of God's kindnesses in your life that you may have forgotten. Mother Teresa worked with the poor on the streets of India for most of her life. She saw first-hand the misery that poverty can bring. At the same time she recognised a different poverty in the Western world, which she called a poverty of spirit—a hunger for love and a hunger for God. This, she said, was a lot more difficult to deal with because she could not alleviate it with medicine, food or shelter. Is part of our poverty that we don't recognise and appreciate how much we have already?

I think that the Bible asks us to remember all of God's benefits because, when we feel rich in blessings and recognise them as gifts from God, we are often more willing to take opportunities available to us, enjoy our lives and share our fortunes with others.

Some years ago I trekked for ten days through the Costa Rican rainforest to raise money for the National Deaf Children's Society. It was tough and, in every sense, a challenge. It started with raising the sponsorship money, included some gruelling hours of training in the gym, and culminated in even more physically demanding trekking through hot and humid forest, scrambling up hills and slipping down rocks. I'm not a natural camper, so the reality of drinking water from streams and living for a week on little more than rice and beans, without showers, flushing lavatories or a comfortable bed, didn't come easily. However, I surprised myself by how simply I could live and how, in many ways, I am much stronger and more capable than I imagined.

I was privileged to be one of only nine fundraisers taking part. This trail through the forest had only been open for a year and we were the fourth group to walk it. The terrain was demanding—through extremely dense cloud forest of bamboo, twisty roots, monkey ferns and huge trees covered in hanging moss—but it was enjoyable because of the many beautiful sights along the way. As we climbed higher to set up camp, we watched mist crawling down over the canopy and the lights of fireflies darting through the trees. My aching feet were a small price to pay for this incredible experience. Removing my boots for the evening, I thought about my friend back home who volunteers for mountain rescue; without his help and advice to get the right gear and equipment, I would have been really struggling. When I looked across at our Costa Rican guide, however, I noticed he was wearing thin-soled shoes. I imagine he must have felt every rough stone under his feet, but he never once complained.

On the final day, we were told that a treat awaited us at the end of our walk—a glass of wine in a cantina. The place turned out to be much the same as pubs the world over, with football on a TV behind the bar, a jukebox and a pool table, but our wine came in randomly shaped glasses, and measures were poured out depending on what glass was clean at the time. Sitting there, I felt lucky to have had such a wonderful experience. I looked down at the boots that carried me and mentally measured my feet against our guide's. Maybe my boots would fit him? He was doing this trail many times a year, so I figured he needed them more than I did.

I took my boots off. 'Would you like these, if they fit you?' I asked.

At first he didn't understand and thought that I was giving them to him to clean. Then he realised they were a gift, and his face radiated such happiness that seeing it made me happy too.

'What about your socks?' he asked.

'My socks?'

'Yes, do you want your socks?'

'You don't want these socks, after I've been walking in them all day. They are dirty,' I said, a little embarrassed.

'They will wash,' he said cheerfully, and so I handed him my socks as well.

We had one night in a hotel before going home and I was very much looking forward to a hot shower when we arrived. The hotel looked like paradise after sharing a two-person tent. I laid my bags down and jumped in the shower. There was no water—not a drop. I went to the sink and tried the tap—nothing. A few years previously I'd had a similar experience when travelling in Peru: if we tried to shower after 6.00 am, the taps ran dry because by that time everyone had used what water there was. Obviously, I'd been beaten to it this time as well, so I put on my bathing suit, walked the two minutes to the sea and watched the sunset on the beach instead.

I remember coming home from that trip, soaking in a bath with fragrant oil and feeling as if it was the most decadent experience in the world. For a short time I really appreciated the small luxuries in my life that I'd taken for granted. It was as if I was seeing everything afresh, as if I'd forgotten how cosy it feels to snuggle under a duvet and wear clean clothes. I'd brought some coffee back with me, and when I drank it I savoured the taste, thinking about all the people I'd seen working on the coffee plantations and in the factories of Costa Rica. I began enjoying my food more, thinking about the variety that is available within a short walking distance of my home, and all the people who work to make that possible. I was benefiting from the work and talents of so many people and yet I'd started to believe that by going to the supermarket, paying for the food and cooking it, I was somehow doing it all myself.

About a month after I returned from my trip, a new outdoor shop opened in Manchester and I was given a £100 voucher to spend instore. Trying on new boots, I thought of our guide in Costa Rica and smiled at how our generosity has a habit of coming back to us in unexpected ways.

TODAY'S PRACTICE

1   Find 15 minutes in your day to sit quietly, close your eyes, take in a couple of deep breaths to help you relax, and be still in the presence of God. Imagine you are breathing in God's love and breathing out anything that is troubling you.

2   If we look at the etymology for the words 'thank' and 'think', we find they have the same origin. Saying, 'Thank you' used to mean, 'I think of you' or 'I will remember what you did for me.' As you go through your day, recognise and say thank you to God for all his benefits, large and small. To start off,

simply think about everything you use as part of your morning routine—soap, water, toothbrush, toothpaste, towel and so on. In just these few minutes of your day, you are benefiting from a lot of other people's work and talents. Ask God to help you appreciate all of his kindnesses, so that in recognising how much you already have, you feel confident to reach out and spread his generosity by asking who you can bless in return.

3 At the end of the day, spend five minutes thinking about any good things that have happened and things that you have enjoyed. Fill the space for today's diary entry. Don't stop writing until the space is full. It doesn't matter how big or small the thing is that you choose to write down. All that matters is that you are noting something good that happened today. When you have written your list, thank God for all the things that are on it.

SEE YOURSELF AS GOD SEES YOU

'You are the light of the world. A town built on a hill cannot be hidden. Neither do people light a lamp and put it under a bowl. Instead they put it on its stand, and it gives light to everyone in the house. In the same way, let your light shine before others, that they may see your good deeds and glorify your Father in heaven.'

MATTHEW 5:14–16

I recently saw a newspaper headline that read, 'Brave college student ditches make-up for an entire year.' Wow, that must have taken some courage! OK, as you might have guessed, my tongue was firmly in my cheek as I made that comment. Seriously, though, Anna Garau, a 20-year-old from Indiana University, made international news with her experiment, and women everywhere began talking about how long they thought they could go without wearing make-up. I wear make-up myself, but, the way I look at it, if being seen without it is such a big problem for you, then clearly you are very blessed. On the scale of things that can go wrong in life, running out of mascara doesn't come very high on most people's lists.

I looked at the photograph of Anna published next to her story. In my eyes, she was a pretty young woman. I don't know what kind of mirror Anna has at home, but she said that when she looked in it she saw love handles, a weird nose, pale skin, squinty eyes and thin lips. Those assessments are harsh by anyone's standards. When that's how you're judging yourself, you don't need enemies to put you down.

Perhaps in 20 years Anna will look at the same photo and think, 'Gosh, was I really that beautiful? What on earth was I worried about?' Hopefully, she won't even have to wait that long. A little over halfway through her experiment, she wrote on local news site www.kentucky.com, 'I've learned that some people do treat me differently, but the people who matter don't. I've also learned that I overemphasised how much thought other people gave to my appearance. I've started relying more on my other assets. Working on kindness, humour and positivity has helped me change in meaningful ways.'

Lots of women use make-up as a way to enhance their beauty or to express care about their appearance. Unfortunately, Anna was using it to hide or change who she was. I don't think it was ditching make-up that made the difference to her outlook. It was learning to accept herself, not as she would like to be but as she is right now.

Some people never begin to accept themselves. Instead, they live their whole lives trying to be the person they think other people want them to be. They look in the mirror and, instead of seeing what is good about themselves, they focus on what they wish was different. Rather than looking at their life as a whole and celebrating their gifts and talents, they look at someone else and ask, 'Why aren't I like that?' or 'Why can't I do that?' or 'Why haven't I got that?'

Most of the time, feelings of dislike towards ourselves aren't deliberate. After all, would you willingly encourage someone who constantly criticised you to follow you around all day, every day? I know I wouldn't. I also know that that is exactly how I've behaved towards myself in the past. I've sometimes said things to myself about myself that I would never dream of thinking, let alone saying, about a friend or anyone else.

The Bible is full of stories about people who doubted their abilities or, in others' eyes, didn't make the grade. When God called them, he knew their past and their shortcomings, but he also knew what they are capable of. He didn't wait for them to reach a certain level of holiness before they could do his work; he met them where they were and gave them a call that would lead them to become the kind of person he knew they were all along.

You are not the same as the next person, but that doesn't mean that you are right and he is wrong, or that he is right and you are wrong. As Paul eloquently puts it, 'The sun has one kind of splendour, the moon another and the stars another; and star differs from star in splendour' (1 Corinthians 15:41). We all have a part to play, a destiny to fulfil, but we can't do it if we're busy trying to be someone we're not.

Shortly after Jesus' resurrection, he is having breakfast with his disciples and, after they've eaten, he talks to Peter about what he would like Peter to do. First he asks for Peter's commitment of love and then he says, 'Feed my sheep'. This was his calling to Peter to look after the flock—that is, the Church. Jesus then says to Peter, 'Follow me,' at which point Peter turns and looks towards one of the other disciples, asking, 'Lord, what about him?'

Jesus replies, 'If I want him to remain alive until I return, what is that to you? You must follow me' (John 21:15–22).

I'm sure we've all been like Peter at some point in our lives, looking at what someone else is doing or not doing, and missing the unique call that Jesus has placed on our life. Seeing yourself as God sees you is not about pretending to be someone or something you are not. It is about recognising who, in God's eyes, you already are—your authentic self. You have been 'wonderfully made' (Psalm 139:14). Trust that. Believe you are loved by God and that he has a unique and good plan for your life, that no one else can fulfil.

TODAY'S PRACTICE

1 Find 15 minutes in your day to sit quietly, close your eyes, take in a couple of deep breaths to help you relax, and be still in the presence of God. Imagine you are breathing in God's love and breathing out anything that is troubling you.

2 To accept love and forgive ourselves, as God loves and forgives us, can be very difficult. You might not be where you want to be in life, but we need to start from where we are and what we've got now. Everyone is on a spiritual journey and we need to keep our eyes on Jesus if we are to find the right path. Let your light shine. Imagine there is a string going through the centre of your head and pulling you up towards the sky, and stand tall. Recognise any points in the day when your thoughts become self-critical, and turn them around into something positive. Look in the mirror and remind yourself that you are talented, you are wonderful and you are loved.

3 At the end of the day, spend five minutes thinking about any good things that have happened and things that you have enjoyed. Fill the space for today's diary entry. Don't stop writing until the space is full. It doesn't matter how big or small the thing is that you choose to write down. All that matters is that you are noting something good that happened

today. When you have written your list, thank God for all the things that are on it.

DAY 31

APPRECIATE THE PEOPLE IN YOUR LIFE

Love is patient, love is kind. It does not envy, it does not boast, it is not proud. It does not dishonour others, it is not self-seeking, it is not easily angered, it keeps no record of wrongs. Love does not delight in evil but rejoices with the truth. It always protects, always trusts, always hopes, always perseveres.

1 CORINTHIANS 13:4–7.

As a journalist, I've written about and given my opinion on many subjects, but the most memorable was one for which I had no research to do at all—the subject of how I feel about my mother. Coming up to Mother's Day, my editor thought it would be a nice idea for me to write a piece entitled 'What my mum means to me' and publish it next to an old photo of me as a little girl with my mum.

On the face of it, this should have been the easiest assignment in the world, yet it made me realise how infrequently I stopped to appreciate specific qualities about the people I love. Of course, I love my mother, but *what* did I love about her? That was a whole different question and one that I'd never fully articulated before, not to my mum and not even to myself. Now I was going to do it for the first time in public.

When asked a question like that, I am all too aware how easy it is to slip into platitudes. Such words might be true, but do they reach to the heart of a person? I realised that the idea of the piece, apart from showing an old photo of me to raise a smile, was to make other people think about and appreciate their mothers. I hoped that readers would relate to it, but not in a general way of what it means to be a daughter or a mother. I wasn't writing a piece about mothers; I was writing about *my* mother. If people were to take anything from it, I hoped they would be led to think, if they were given the same task, what would they write? For each person the response would be different.

This is what I wrote:

I hope that my mum already knows what she means to me. After all, she's known me all my life, so I guess I expect her to be able to read my thoughts by now. I say that because, when writing this piece, I realised that I probably haven't told her—not in so many words. Well, over the years I have said a lot, usually starting with, 'Why can't you...? It's your fault...If you'd done...', when really I meant, 'Why can't I...? If I'd only... I'm irritable, I'm frustrated and why can't you wave a magic wand and make everything better, because that's supposed to be a mum's job, isn't it?'

I never admit that, of course. I know I'm being unfair—but, as Mum had a habit of telling me when I was growing up, 'Life's not always fair.' At the same time, she's always encouraged me to share, to look for the good in things, to be generous, to think about situations from the other person's point of view and, to all intents and purposes, try to be fair. No wonder I get confused.

Anyway, for all my whining 'What about me?' I now realise that, since I was born, my mum has always considered me in everything. Even now, she still asks, 'Have you eaten?' and if I misplace something she has an uncanny knack of working out where it is without setting a foot through the door.

And it's not just me. My mum has spent her life looking after other people. As well as working full-time and caring for our home and family, Mum makes weekly visits to the elderly and those in hospital who have no relatives nearby. I often hear about her acts of kindness from others, years later. Mum doesn't think anything of it. She says, 'Surely anyone would do the same?' I don't know how she's got to her age without realising that they wouldn't.

My mum is full of life and always on the go. She can't even walk from the car to the house without pulling out a stray weed from the garden. She makes me laugh more than anyone—not always intentionally. We chat on the phone every day because, as well as my mum, she's also my friend and I want to share my day with her.

Come to think of it, perhaps I've never told my mum what she means to me because, like here, my words seem so inadequate. They get jumbled somewhere between my heart and my mouth. Or maybe it's just that sometimes emotions are bigger than the language we have to express them. So, to keep it simple, I love you, Mum. You mean everything to me that is good, and don't let anything I might say ever let you believe otherwise.

The headline on the story read, 'Telling your mum how special she is means more than any gift'. Of course, I still sent a Mother's Day card and bought a present for my mum that year. Presents and cards are tokens of appreciation, but it is the appreciation that is the real gift, greater than any money can buy. Real appreciation is what strengthens relationships, because it benefits not only the person who is appreciated but also the person who shows appreciation.

When we are close to people, it can be easy to take for

granted all the things we love about them, and, unless we are careful, we can end up focusing on those things about them that irritate us. As our scripture passage for today highlights, love focuses on the positive and chooses to see and appreciate the best in people. When we appreciate people, we automatically feel more love towards them and, as a result, we are more patient, kind, generous and forgiving.

It is eight years since I wrote that piece, and what I learned from doing it has improved my relationship not only with my mum but with all the people in my life. I haven't written newspaper articles about all of them, but I do regularly take time to remind myself what I love most about them and the ways in which they enrich my life. As a result, their good qualities are always foremost in my mind, even when we disagree. I try to be quick to thank my family and friends for things they do for me—things that I may at one time have taken for granted—and to thank God for all the people and love he has brought into my life.

TODAY'S PRACTICE

1 Find 15 minutes in your day to sit quietly, close your eyes, take in a couple of deep breaths to help you relax, and be still in the presence of God. Imagine you are breathing in God's love and breathing out anything that is troubling you.

2 Think about a person in your life whom you love. If you had to write something about what they mean to you, what would you say? What are this person's best qualities? What is it you love about them? Offer a prayer of thanks to God for bringing this person into your life. In all your relationships, take any

opportunities to express your appreciation for the love and support people give you. It can be as simple as saying thank you if someone helps you out in any way, such as giving you a ride in their car, calling to see how you are, accompanying you to the doctors, cooking you a meal or doing the housework.

3 At the end of the day, spend five minutes thinking about any good things that have happened and things that you have enjoyed. Fill the space for today's diary entry. Don't stop writing until the space is full. It doesn't matter how big or small the thing is that you choose to write down. All that matters is that you are noting something good that happened today. When you have written your list, thank God for all the things that are on it.

DAY 32

BE YOUR BEST

Whatever you do, work at it with all your heart, as working for the Lord, not for human masters.

COLOSSIANS 3:23

My family and I were out walking our dog when our attention was drawn to a man cleaning the metal barrier that faces out on to the canal. There are six bars between the ground and the top of the barrier, and he cleaned and polished the bottom bar with as much care and attention as he did the top. Although we watched him from a distance as we passed by, there was no one with authority looking over the man's shoulder to make sure he'd done a thorough job. Some people might say that he was cleaning the barrier, only to have a seagull drop mess on it a couple of hours later, but he clearly didn't feel that way about his work. He put a love and care into it that was visible to anyone watching.

Later, I thought again about that man and how, by his attitude to his work and his desire to do the best job he could, he not only made the place cleaner and more pleasant for everyone who passed by that day, but he also inspired us and whoever else saw him. He demonstrated love in his work, and all who looked on could see the value in it.

I wonder what the world would look like if we all poured such love into our work, without cutting corners because... well, everyone does that, don't they? What difference would it make if we stopped putting jobs into categories (like 'important' work and 'menial' work), and if we learned to value each other more, to recognise our interdependence and see each role as important in making life more comfortable and enjoyable for everyone?

If you think that's idealistic nonsense, think about how different it feels at work if one person doesn't pull their weight, if a colleague complains all the time about how bad the job is, if the server at the kiosk is surly, if a barman serves you a drink in a dirty glass, if your doctor talks about you as if you're a body part and not a person, or if your waiter is rude. Turn all those experiences into positive ones, and the day suddenly becomes a lot easier for everyone.

People spend, on average, a third of their day at work. Unfortunately, though, for most people it isn't a satisfying experience. If you don't enjoy your job or you feel undervalued at work, you are far from alone. Global research company Gallup published a poll of 25 million employees across 189 different countries, which showed the same results the world over. Internationally, only 13 per cent of respondents reported having any sense of passion for their work or connection to their employer. Of the rest, 63 per cent said they were unhappy and put very little energy into their job, while 24 per cent were what Gallup called 'actively disengaged'—meaning that they were so dissatisfied, they took out their frustration on others by deliberately disrupting and undermining their work.[13]

Amy Wrzesniewski, Professor of Organisational Behaviour at Yale School of Management, has published numerous studies on how people make meaning of their work in difficult contexts—for example, if they work in stigmatised occupations. She has shown that people will readily categorise their employment as either a job (where they are in it for the money), a career (where their main interest is advancement and prestige) or a calling (which many of us might think of as a vocation or a passion). Interestingly, in all occupations there were people who fell into each of the three categories, and, when a separate analysis was carried out on a sample of administrative assistants, the percentages who fell within each of the three categories—job, career or calling—were roughly the same as emerged for the sample as a whole. Through her study, Professor Wrzesniewski has come to believe that satisfaction with life and with work may be more dependent on how an employee sees his or her work than on income or occupational prestige.[14]

Of course, it can be difficult to maintain a good attitude at work if you are surrounded by people who fall into the 24 per cent of colleagues who are deliberatively disruptive and make life difficult for other people in the workplace. I have had experiences like this myself. When I was younger I worked in an office where many people came in and left without expressing the common courtesy of saying 'hello' or 'goodbye'. After a while, I stopped greeting colleagues as well, but the lack of connection began to get me down. Then I remembered a story my dad used to tell me when I was at school. It was about a man who said a cheerful 'Good morning' as he walked past the same man on his walk to work every day. He never once got a response.

One day another man said to him, 'I've heard you greet that man every day and he's never once acknowledged you. Why do you continue to do it?'

The man replied, 'Because I'm not going to let someone else's attitude influence my behaviour.'

Are you letting other people's attitudes affect your behaviour? Would your attitude to work change if you knew you were working for God?

I've heard many people say that a Christian never retires because God's work for us here is never done. Once we realise that our deeper vocation is to love, we can find satisfaction in whatever work we are doing, because there is an opportunity to love in every situation.

TODAY'S PRACTICE

1 Find 15 minutes in your day to sit quietly, close your eyes, take in a couple of deep breaths to help you relax, and be still in the presence of God. Imagine you are breathing in God's love and breathing out anything that is troubling you.

2 Whatever work you do today, whether it is paid, voluntary or essential tasks in the home, give it your best effort. Focus on the good things about your work and think about how you could do it with more care, attention and love.

3 At the end of the day, spend five minutes thinking about any good things that have happened and things that you have enjoyed. Fill the space for today's diary entry. Don't stop writing until the space is full. It doesn't matter how big or small the thing is that you choose to write down. All that matters is that you are noting something good that happened today. When you have written your list, thank God for all the things that are on it.

ENJOY YOUR LIFE

Our mouths were filled with laughter, our tongues with songs of joy. Then it was said among the nations, 'The Lord has done great things for them.'

PSALM 126:2

When the Manchester International Festival, held biennially in my home town, commissioned the Young@Heart Chorus from Massachusetts, USA, and No Theatre to produce a new show called *End of the Road*, I was invited to the premiere. If I'm honest, when I saw the advertising flyer, I realised it wasn't something that I would have chosen to see. The festival programme was bursting with new work from international talent, like Cuban ballet dancer Carlos Acosta, performance artist Marina Abramović, and singer-songwriter Rufus Wainwright. Compared with what else was on offer, it seemed I had drawn the short straw—a retirement home choir, with an average age of 84, singing about getting to the end of the road. Even the novelty factor of seeing people in their 90s singing punk rock couldn't overcome my initial reservations. I fully expected to come out feeling a little bit maudlin.

It's nice to be surprised. There was something unexpectedly moving about the performance: familiar songs from recent decades were being sung by people whose life experiences gave the lyrics a different emphasis and, in many ways, a deeper meaning. The audience jumped to their feet as one at the curtain call, not just a couple of people standing and the rest deciding to join them in dribs and drabs. The applause was spontaneous and energised—the kind of reaction that you can't ignore because it rushes through your whole body and demands a response, whether cheers, whistles, applause or simply a big wide grin. It was a response that only comes from watching people truly enjoy themselves— joy responding to joy.

Afterwards I chatted with one of the chorus members, Dora Morrow, who was 87 years old at the time. I couldn't have been more excited had I been meeting a pop star. Who would have thought, at her age, that she would be travelling around the world, performing in front of huge crowds? She had certainly never imagined that this could happen in her life, and she was determined to enjoy every moment of it.

Dora's daughter, one of her 15 children, was travelling with her. Her son-in-law was the drummer for the Young@ Heart band and had initially encouraged her to go along to a chorus rehearsal to get her out of the house to start mixing with people again after her husband, Lewis, died. Seven years later, Dora was very much a part of the group, rehearsing for two hours, twice a week, joining the chorus on international tours and, more than anything, having fun.

Another of the singers, Glenda Philips, described her experience in the chorus as 'a joyride'. As a young woman she had always held dreams of being a performer but had never pursued them. 'Now look at me,' she said. 'It's just a miracle. I don't believe I'm up there.' I wonder how many more miracles would be open to us if we let go of all our preconceptions about what we should and shouldn't, or can and cannot do, at certain ages—if we let ourselves be free to enjoy life.

Little children know this instinctively. My two-year-old nephew brings joy wherever he goes, because he is so filled with joy himself. He sings and dances with abandon. He hollers across the road with excitement to greet someone he knows, and when he eats something he likes, he closes his eyes to savour the taste of it. At his age, everything is new and exciting. Last week he ran into the room after my brother had been shopping. 'Wow, look at the size of this banana!' he said, holding the piece of fruit up in front of me enthusiastically. Come to think of it, it was amazing—not only how the banana had grown on a plant thousands of miles away, but the number of people who'd been involved in harvesting the fruit, packaging it and transporting it, so that we could walk to the end of the street and pick it off a shelf. To us, that is ordinary, but for a short moment I allowed myself to be amazed too, and to share my nephew's excitement.

How can we hold on to that excitement, that joy for life, which seems to get lost under a weight of responsibility as we get older? There is no one answer, but if we want to have a more enjoyable and exciting life, we need to make time to do things that we enjoy. We need to be willing to be excited, stay open to opportunities and recognise the wonder of experiences we've grown used to.

The man who holds Young@Heart together, and the talent behind its musical arrangements, is Bob Cilman. He founded the group in 1982, when he was working at a centre serving meals to elderly people on low incomes. He was approached by Judith Sharpe, a woman in her 60s, who offered to play the piano for him, and he thought a sing-along might be a good idea to break the routine. Bob was 29 years old at the time and, more than 30 years later, he is still working with the chorus alongside his day job as Director of the Northampton Arts Council. To stick with it that long shows not only a real dedication on his part; it is also a commitment of love. I get the impression that the chorus would continue to meet and sing, whether it had an audience or not. Could our lives be more enjoyable if we simply committed more to those activities that bring us joy?

Laugher and joy are infectious. Of course, your enthusiasm won't always be welcomed by everyone. There will always be people who try to put down, even in the smallest of ways, the things you enjoy. But if you're committed to enjoying your life, you will be able to brush off these comments more easily. There will always be people who tell you you're too old to do this, or you don't have the talent to do that. Don't fall into the trap of turning down an opportunity to learn something new by reasoning, 'Well, I can't do that, because do you know how old I'll be by the time I can do it?' Whatever your age, the answer is always the same: 'Yes, the same age you'll be if you don't even try.'

TODAY'S PRACTICE

1 Find 15 minutes in your day to sit quietly, close your eyes, take in a couple of deep breaths to help you relax, and be still in the presence of God. Imagine you are breathing in God's love and breathing out anything that is troubling you.

2 Make a list of ten things that you enjoy doing. How long is it since you did any of them? Choose one that you haven't done for a long time, set a date to do it, and stick to it. Make another list of things you think you might enjoy and would like to try. Think about your dreams as a child. Perhaps, like

Glenda, you had dreams of being a singer. Could you join a choir? If you dreamt of being a dancer, could you join a dance class or go and watch a show? Choose something from your list and think about different ways that you could reignite that dream and the excitement within yourself.

3 At the end of the day, spend five minutes thinking about any good things that have happened and things that you have enjoyed. Fill the space for today's diary entry. Don't stop writing until the space is full. It doesn't matter how big or small the thing is that you choose to write down. All that matters is that you are noting something good that happened today. When you have written your list, thank God for all the things that are on it.

DECIDE TO BE HAPPY

For as he thinks within himself, so he is.
PROVERBS 23:7

I once worked with a company director who was cheerful all the time—or at least that was the image he portrayed. I spent time with him in and out of work because he was good to be around. Having him in the workplace lightened the mood. He worked hard, and I was always willing to go the extra mile on his projects. I didn't find the extra work stressful because, as a boss, he created a relaxed atmosphere simply by being pleasant. Although I liked his attitude, I found it unusual for someone to be so consistently happy, especially at work. What was his secret? So one day in the canteen I asked him, 'How come you always seem so happy? What is it that you do?'

He looked at me and recognised that I wasn't being sarcastic. 'Happiness is a choice,' he said, 'and I choose to be happy.'

Until then I'd never thought of being happy as a choice. I wasn't sure I could simply choose to be happy, but here was a man who said that is what he did, and who was I to say it was rubbish? Clearly the choice was making some difference in his life, because I had noticed his unusually upbeat attitude and everyone around him benefited from it, even if they didn't say so.

It was some years later when I heard the same claim

again. I was watching a TV film called *Marvellous*, a true story about a man called Neil Baldwin, a former Stoke City FC kit-man, whose philosophy of life is 'I've always wanted to be happy, so I decided to be.' Neil, who makes several cameo appearances in the film as himself, is such a warm-hearted and genuine character that when he tells us this is his secret in life, we have no choice but to believe him. His philosophy seems a childlike view of the world, but there is no mistaking that it has worked for Neil.

Neil was 68 years old when the film was released, and, had his life story been fiction, it would probably have been deemed too far-fetched to portray. His adventures include joining the circus, drinking sherry with British royalty, taking a regular seat on the official launch for the Oxford and Cambridge boat race, playing in a friendly match for Stoke City, running his own football team, and taking afternoon tea with several archbishops. When Neil was awarded an honorary degree at Keele University, where he had unofficially appointed himself as a greeter 50 years earlier, it turned into a two-day celebration, with speeches from distinguished alumni, a formal dinner, a testimonial football match and a service of thanksgiving for his work, conducted by his good friend the Bishop of Lichfield. Then, to top it all, he had a film made about him. No wonder he is happy, you might say, but that would certainly be too simplistic.

While Neil's philosophy on life may seem simple, his life circumstances have not been ideal. When he was a boy, he was diagnosed with learning difficulties, although he has never considered himself to be disadvantaged in any way. His father died when Neil was very young. Neil has no siblings and he grew up with his mother, who was a great support but who also often worried if Neil would be able to manage in the world on his own.

Neil has met his share of unpleasant people, but, the way he sees it, there will always be some bad people in the world, and, if you just walk away, a good person will come along soon enough. Lou Macari, the Stoke City manager who hired Neil, later described him as the best signing he'd ever made. He attributed much of the club's success at that time to Neil's sense of fun, which lifted the morale of the team. Neil is not happy because wonderful things have happened in his life. Rather, it seems that wonderful things have happened because he is happy.

At this point you might be thinking, 'Well, you don't know what is going on in my life. It's not that simple. I can't just choose to be happy.' In the past, I have thought the same way. Yet, people who have a happy outlook say otherwise, and there is a body of scientific research called 'positive psychology' to back them up. Researchers studying identical twins brought up in different environments say that our genes determine 50 per cent of our happiness, and that we all have a happiness 'set point' at which we'll settle, regardless of what happens to us.[15] Yet, while our happiness is genetically influenced, it is not genetically fixed. Our circumstances, including our job, financial situation, social status and health, surprisingly account for only ten per cent of our happiness. There is another 40 per cent that is determined by intentional activities—things we can do each day to help raise our happiness, like spending time in silence, being thankful, focusing on the good in life, helping other people, looking after a pet, taking care of the environment, spending time with friends and family, or varying our activities.

Knowing this makes me realise just how much wisdom

there is in the pages of the Bible, which we can easily overlook because we think, 'Surely life isn't that straightforward?'

The apostle Paul didn't need statistics to help him understand the elusive secret of happiness. He writes that he has learned to be content, no matter what his circumstances (Philippians 4:11). Paul knew that if we wait for all of our circumstances to be just as we want them to be before we can feel peaceful and happy, we will be waiting for a very long time. Anything we learn takes practice. We can't expect to decide to be happy and see an instant transformation in our level of contentment, but we can begin to change our thoughts, to focus on the good, to put love first and to lean on God. We can ask for his strength not merely to overcome our problems but to be content and able to experience joy even in the midst of them.

TODAY'S PRACTICE

1 Find 15 minutes in your day to sit quietly, close your eyes, take in a couple of deep breaths to help you relax, and be still in the presence of God. Imagine you are breathing in God's love and breathing out anything that is troubling you.

2 Many people think it is unrealistic to expect good things to happen in life, but why is it more realistic to assume the opposite? We know that the majority of bad events we worry about never actually happen to us. Today, notice when you have discouraging thoughts and consciously change them to focus on encouraging possibilities for your life. Ask God to strengthen you and help you experience his joy by recognising the goodness in every situation.

3 At the end of the day, spend five minutes thinking about any good things that have happened and things that you have

enjoyed. Fill the space for today's diary entry. Don't stop writing until the space is full. It doesn't matter how big or small the thing is that you choose to write down. All that matters is that you are noting something good that happened today. When you have written your list, thank God for all the things that are on it.

DAY 35

REFLECT ON YOUR WEEK

I will give thanks to you, Lord, with all my heart; I will tell of all your wonderful deeds.

PSALM 9:1

There is something freeing that happens when we allow ourselves to feel safe and secure in the knowledge that God loves, accepts and forgives us, and works everything out for good. Once we allow ourselves to truly feel God's love, it's not just our own view in the mirror that begins to change; we begin to mirror his love back to the world.

For the past five weeks you have been keeping a record of good things that have happened in your life. Look back over your notes. Take time to remember some kindnesses that you might have forgotten and to savour the memory of any wonderful moments that have happened in this time. Give thanks to God for all the blessings you have received, big and small.

Looking back over the exercises in the week, what exercises did you most enjoy? Why do you think that was? Did any experiences surprise you? Did any issues arise that you would consider significant? Are there any changes that you would like to make as a result of your experiences this week?

TODAY'S PRACTICE

1 Find 15 minutes in your day to sit quietly, close your eyes, take in a couple of deep breaths to help you relax, and be still in the presence of God. Imagine you are breathing in God's love and breathing out anything that is troubling you.

2 At the end of the day, spend five minutes thinking about any good things that have happened and things that you have enjoyed. Fill the space for today's diary entry. Don't stop writing until the space is full. It doesn't matter how big or small the thing is that you choose to write down. All that matters is that you are noting something good that happened today. When you have written your list, thank God for all the things that are on it.

WEEK 6

BELIEVE IN MIRACLES

Jesus looked at them and said,
'With man this is impossible,
but with God all things are possible.'

MATTHEW 19:26

DAY 36

REMEMBER YOUR MIRACLES

They asked each other, 'Were not our hearts burning within us while he talked with us on the road and opened the Scriptures to us?' They got up and returned at once to Jerusalem. There they found the Eleven and those with them, assembled together and saying, 'It is true! The Lord has risen and has appeared to Simon.'

LUKE 24:32–34

My favourite place in the world is the Northumberland coast, in the north-east of England. The area remains largely untouched commercially and you can sometimes walk the full stretch of a beach without seeing another soul. My parents live about half an hour's drive away from the coast and, as a child, I visited the seaside frequently, summer and winter. We still often go for coastal walks when I'm home, and it never stops feeling like a treat. The light is very special there, bright and clear. The air has a nip in it but it's crisp and fresh, carrying a faint but unmistakable scent of salt water. The beaches are sandy, rather than pebble or shale, and I like to feel the soft sand on my feet, to hear the sound of the waves breaking on the shore and to look out across miles and miles of sea to the horizon. There is a power to the sea that I find fascinating. In one sense it's always the same, but in another it's forever changing—constantly moving and full of energy that inspires in me both awe and calm in equal measures. Perhaps I find it a spiritually nourishing place because the way I feel when I'm looking out to sea is how I think about my relationship with God.

There is nothing static or dull about a living faith, and yet in recent times the image of a Christian seems to have lost some of its vitality. For many, it suggests a list of 'do not do's' rather than an expression of a joyous life, lived in all its fullness. It is almost as if we know that Jesus is risen but we don't allow ourselves to feel it in our hearts.

I was baptised within a month of my birth and grew up in a Christian home. As many cradle Christians will know, it is easy to become so familiar with the message of Jesus that we cease to be excited by it. I recently met a young woman called Kelly, who had started learning about Jesus only in the past year. She was in her early 20s but her difficult life experiences had weighed heavily on her, giving her the appearance and outlook of someone much older. By her own account, she never used to smile. Hearing Kelly tell her story, it was difficult to imagine the person she used to be, because when I met her she never stopped smiling. Indeed, she radiated a joy that was not only visible, it was infectious.

Kelly told me that after being bereaved of three people close to her, including her partner, who died from alcohol-related illness, she had found it difficult to cope. She had lost all confidence in herself and in other people. Most days she couldn't even muster up the energy to get out of bed. But one day she was surprised to find herself offloading her troubles on the local vicar, Jimmy.

Aside from times, as a young child, when she attended services with her school, Kelly had only ever been inside a church for funerals. As she stood outside the church after the third family funeral she had attended in a matter of months, Jimmy noticed her despair and offered a listening ear. At that time, Kelly knew nothing about Jesus. Curious, she began asking Jimmy questions, and he gave her a book to take home and read.

She was bursting with enthusiasm as she told me how she started attending church because she longed to know more about this man, Jesus, who loved unconditionally and was accepting of all people, irrespective of their faults. In Jesus' message, Kelly found hope—hope that she could move on and have a good life; hope that she was lovable and loved no matter what had gone before. Sometimes it's good to be reminded in this way just how good the good news of the gospel is.

It's the same with everything in life. Once something or someone becomes familiar and routine, we can allow these amazing blessings on our life to become ordinary. I became aware of that most acutely when I watched a story on the news about Joanne Milne from Gateshead, Tyne and Wear, who, because of advances in medical technology, became able to hear sounds for the first time at the age of 39.

Joanne has Usher Syndrome, a rare genetic disorder resulting in a combination of hearing loss and visual impairment. She was born deaf and her sight has gradually deteriorated since her 20s, so she now has tunnel vision and is registered blind. Improvements in technology meant there was a chance that surgery could help her to hear, so Joanne underwent an operation to insert cochlear implants behind each ear. These are electronic medical devices that replace the function of the damaged inner ear by stimulating the auditory nerve to send sound signals to the brain. After the operation, Joanne had to wait a month before the implants were switched on, to find out if the surgery had been a success. Her mother travelled with her to the Queen

Elizabeth Hospital in Birmingham, where the procedure had been carried out, and filmed Joanne's reaction as her cochlear implants were turned on and she heard a human voice for the first time.

That two-minute film clip went viral. In later interviews, Joanne talked about the joy of hearing sounds like the ping of a light switch and running water, sounds so ordinary to most of us that we barely notice them. She told the *Daily Mail*, 'It was emotional, exciting, amazing. I was so happy. I hadn't imagined it would be so wonderful and I wanted to savour every moment. I didn't want it to pass too quickly. A little voice in my head was saying, "This is what sound is like", and it all surprised me.'

So often we can overlook amazing gifts, even the miracle of life itself, because these gifts are so natural to us. Is there something in your life that you need be turned on to again? There are wonders all around us if we open ourselves to recognise them.

TODAY'S PRACTICE

1 Find 15 minutes in your day to sit quietly, close your eyes, take in a couple of deep breaths to help you relax, and be still in the presence of God. Imagine you are breathing in God's love and breathing out anything that is troubling you.

2 Are there things in your life that once seemed like a miracle but have now become routine? Think about something that you possess, or have achieved, that at one time felt like an amazing blessing. It could be a child, a relationship, a new house, a new job, an adventure, a new skill or an opportunity. Remind yourself what it felt like when that blessing first came into your

life. Turn on your original enthusiasm, excitement and joy, remembering how blessed it once made you feel. Thank God for these blessings.

3 At the end of the day, spend five minutes thinking about any good things that have happened and things that you have enjoyed. Fill the space for today's diary entry. Don't stop writing until the space is full. It doesn't matter how big or small the thing is that you choose to write down. All that matters is that you are noting something good that happened today. When you have written your list, thank God for all the things that are on it.

DAY 37

BE THE MIRACLE

'For I was hungry and you gave me something to eat, I was thirsty and you gave me something to drink, I was a stranger and you invited me in, I needed clothes and you clothed me, I was ill and you looked after me, I was in prison and you came to visit me.'

MATTHEW 25:35–36

When we look back over our lives, we can all remember incidents when someone seemed to show up at just the right time. Had they come into our lives minutes later or earlier, events could have turned out very different for us. 'What a lucky coincidence,' we'll often say. Sometimes, the kindness shown is so important to us that we describe that person as an angel.

I was thinking about this after a friend recalled the events of a day trip with his family. They were enjoying a country walk when his mother-in-law suddenly fell ill. It was a remote spot and none of them could get a phone signal to call for help. Within a couple of minutes, a young woman came down the hill. As it turned out, she was a medic and recognised immediately what was wrong. 'We had seen no one all day, and then she showed up out of the blue when we needed someone,' my friend said. 'It was like she was an angel.'

In that woman's kindness my friend and his family saw a reflection of the divine that is within all of us. To me, that is the essence of the parable of the sheep and the goats. When Jesus says, 'Truly I tell you, whatever you did for one of the least of these brothers and sisters of mine, you did for me' (Matthew 25:40), it's because, in acting out our faith, not only are we recognising the divine in others, but we are also recognising the divine in ourselves. We are giving life to God's Spirit within us and revealing his love through our actions. Teresa of Avila summed it up when she said, 'Christ has no body now on earth but yours—no hands but yours, no feet but yours. Yours are the hands by which he is to bless us now.'

Our acts of kindness may seem insignificant to us, but we often don't see the impact that they can have on the lives of others. The late American novelist Edison Marshall shared a wonderful example of this from his own life, which I first read as told by Fulton Oursler in his book, *Modern Parables*.[16]

In 1931, at the height of the Great Depression, Edison was travelling alone on a 400-mile journey when he stopped to give a ride to a young hitchhiker who was standing shivering at the side of the road. As he drove off, he noticed another youth standing in a doorway, barefoot and without a coat, his arms wrapped tightly around his body to keep warm. Edison asked his travelling companion if he knew the cold young man. He was told that, yes, they were friends and were both travelling that way for a job but had imagined it would be too difficult to get a lift together, as drivers might see two youths together as a threat. Edison was tempted to turn back, but, anxious to get to his destination on time, decided against it. His conscience continued to nag at him, though, so he decided to ask the tollhouse keeper at the next toll if he could leave some money for the young man to collect as he passed through. At least that way the kid could buy himself a coat or shoes—something to help him keep warm.

Edison greeted the tollhouse keeper with a cheerful 'Hello', but the man offered no reply. Nevertheless, before driving off, Edison decided to risk asking for a favour from the grouchy old man and handed him some notes for the youngster.

It was another two years before Edison drove that way again. This time, at the same toll booth, he was greeted by a cheerful grey-haired woman, who thanked him and smiled as he handed over the coin for his toll. Curious, he asked her if it had been her husband who was on duty when he drove through two years earlier, and if the young man he had left some money for ever showed up.

On hearing his question, the old woman grabbed his hand warmly. 'So you're the one!' she said. 'My husband wasn't nice to you, was he? He wasn't nice to anyone for years and years. I could understand, because it was hard on me too. You see, we lost our boy in the big war. He was our only one. Pop was never the same after—not until the morning that young fellow came here and Pop handed him your money. Somehow they got talking. We gave him some coffee, and before we'd finished Pop invited Roy to stay with us for a while. He did, too. He stayed with us, and he helped out with the work, right up to the time Pop passed away. Wasn't that nice of him? It just meant everything to Pop. Roy, he said, was sent from God to help our lonesomeness. He's up to town now, buying us some fertiliser for the west field— as handsome a son as anyone could want. You could never guess what you did for us all.'

That is how it is with God. When we answer his call to act out our faith, we never know the full impact of our actions. What seems a small act to us could be part of a miracle that God is working in someone else's life.

TODAY'S PRACTICE

1 Find 15 minutes in your day to sit quietly, close your eyes, take in a couple of deep breaths to help you relax, and be still in the presence of God. Imagine you are breathing in God's love and breathing out anything that is troubling you.

2 When we think about doing something that will make a positive difference to someone else's life, it can feel very daunting. We can allow ourselves to get disheartened because, in the great scheme of things, our kindness can feel insignificant. However, we never know how God will use our actions. Jesus said, 'By this everyone will know that you are my disciples, if you love one another' (John 13:35). Today, imagine that you are rooted in love. View all people with the eyes of love, and let your actions flow from it.

3 At the end of the day, spend five minutes thinking about any good things that have happened and things that you have enjoyed. Fill the space for today's diary entry. Don't stop writing until the space is full. It doesn't matter how big or small the thing is that you choose to write down. All that matters is that you are noting something good that happened today. When you have written your list, thank God for all the things that are on it.

SEE THE DIVINE EVERYWHERE

Jesus did many other things as well. If every one of them were written down, I suppose that even the whole world would not have room for the books that would be written.

JOHN 21:25

There is a walkway on the Argentinian side of the Iguazu Falls in South America, which leads through the rainforest of the national park to the top of the falls. By this, I don't mean that it takes you to a postcard view of the falls. There are other trails for that purpose. Here you walk along a narrow metal bridge over the falls, where you stand on the rim of a horseshoe shaped precipice, watching a rush of water pouring in from three sides. This part of the falls is called *Garganta del Diablo*, or Devil's Throat. Looking down, you can't see the water below because of a huge chasm full of mist and spray, thrown up by the rush of the falls. Perhaps the early settlers imagined falling in and being swallowed into the centre of the earth, never to be seen again. If you look straight ahead, there are waterfalls as far as you can see, 275 of them over a span of 2.7 km, while rainbows hover above and within the mist in every direction.

I remember leaning forward to let the spray hit my face and sensing a stillness that comes from being completely absorbed. It was one of those occasions when language feels inadequate. It was as if my senses were so overwhelmed by the experience that I had no room left for thought.

We've all had those moments—times when we've suddenly felt aware of a power far greater than ourselves, when all we can do is stand in awe and allow the experience to flow through us. Such wondrous glimpses can turn our lives around by opening our eyes to life in a different way. For this reason it can be good to refresh ourselves spiritually by going on a pilgrimage or spending time on retreat. Once back in the routine of our day-to-day lives, however, it can be easy to slip into the perception that God is distant and that we need to travel to feel close to him. The challenge is to keep our eyes open to the divine presence in all of life, wherever we are.

Shortly after Jesus' resurrection, he appeared to his disciples next to the Sea of Tiberias. It happened while the disciples were out fishing (John 21:1–14). For me, living in an urban area, that setting presents a very pleasant picture in my mind. However, when reading the passage, I need to remind myself that for the disciples this activity was nothing out of the ordinary. Peter was a fisherman. It was a job he'd given up to follow Jesus. After Jesus' resurrection he had returned to the day-to-day life he knew before.

For Peter, being out on a boat was the same as it is for me to be sitting in front of a computer screen, typing on a keyboard. Some days, I feel I've achieved more than others. On this particular day, Peter and the disciples have put in a lot of effort with nothing to show for it and have returned after a whole night's fishing, with empty nets. In the morning, as they reach the shore, Jesus is standing on the beach and shouts to them, 'Have you caught anything?' On hearing their disheartened reply, he suggests that if they cast their net on the other side of the boat they'll find something there. As they do as he suggests, the net fills with fish—153 of them. It is only then, as John is hauling in the net, that he recognises the man on the shore as Jesus. He turns and tells Peter, who leaps into the water in his haste to greet the risen Lord.

On the beach, Jesus has set up a charcoal fire on which he's cooking some fish and bread. He invites the disciples to bring some of the fish they've just caught, and then he cooks their breakfast. It is a practical act that shows care for his friends, who will no doubt have been hungry and tired after fishing all night. It is a meal of simple foods that they will have eaten many times before. For the disciples, this is ordinary everyday business. Everything is familiar—friends, surroundings and food. What is extraordinary is that it is here, amid the routine of the day, that Jesus, the risen Lord, chooses to reveal himself.

Often it is easier to sense a spiritual connection in the magnificence of a mountain range, in the cry of a newborn baby or in the vastness of the night sky. Yet Jesus also calls us to recognise and reach out to him right now, wherever we are. When we are tired, when we are hungry, when our work seems unproductive, and when we least expect it, if we allow him to, Jesus will reveal the extraordinary in the midst of our most ordinary routines.

TODAY'S PRACTICE

1 Find 15 minutes in your day to sit quietly, close your eyes, take in a couple of deep breaths to help you relax, and be still in the presence of God. Imagine you are breathing in God's love and breathing out anything that is troubling you.

2 We all have opportunities to experience God every day, but many of us are so caught up in routine activities that it is only when we step out of them that we are able to feel a sense of spiritual connection. Today, take every opportunity to seek God in routine tasks such as cooking, cleaning or gardening. It is in the actions of our everyday life that our strongest relationships are formed, and our relationship with God is no different in this respect. Ask God to help you recognise the divine in yourself, in others and in the world around you. Listen to your heart and be open to where his Spirit is calling you this day.

3 At the end of the day, spend five minutes thinking about any good things that have happened and things that you have enjoyed. Fill the space for today's diary entry. Don't stop writing until the space is full. It doesn't matter how big or small the thing is that you choose to write down. All that matters is that you are noting something good that happened today. When you have written your list, thank God for all the things that are on it.

DAY 39

LIVE WITH HOPE

'I have told you these things, so that in me you may have peace. In this world you will have trouble. But take heart! I have overcome the world.'
JOHN 16:33

Perhaps it is the English tendency to favour the underdog, but ever since I was a child I've been drawn to the biblical story of David and Goliath (1 Samuel 17). At its simplest level, it tells of a mighty warrior defeated by a lowly shepherd boy— an unlikely tale, which has become a common metaphor for 'the little guy wins'. Like all Bible stories, though, this short text contains much more than first appears, and it continues to fascinate generation after generation, who find new meaning in it depending on the circumstances they face. For me, right now, David and Goliath reveals, in a very practical way, what it means to live in hope.

The story begins with a stand-off between two armies separated by a valley, the Philistines on one side of the hills and the Israelites on the other. Goliath steps forward from the Philistine army and challenges the Israelites to send a man to fight him and settle the battle by single combat: whoever is still standing at the end of the challenge, that man's people will have won the battle. Even though the story is told briefly, great detail is given in the description of Goliath. We are told that he stands at six cubits and a span tall, which converts to 9 feet and 9 inches—a giant even by today's standards. The tallest person in recorded history, as listed in the Guinness World Records, was Robert Pershing Wadlow from Illinois, USA, whose height measured 8 feet and 11.1 inches before his death at the age of 22.

So, here is Goliath, head and shoulders above anyone else. To give an idea of his strength, we're told not only about each piece of bronze armour he is wearing, but also the weight of his armour and weaponry—the head of his spear alone weighing 600 shekels of iron, the equivalent of 7 kg or 15 lb of solid metal. As soon as the Israelites see this man, they all run away, terrified—everyone, that is, except a young shepherd boy called David.

When King Saul hears that there is a man willing to face the wrath of Goliath, he sends for David—only to be dismayed. 'You are not able to go out against this Philistine and fight him; you are only a young man, and he has been a warrior from his youth,' he says (v. 33). But David doesn't see either himself or Goliath in the way everyone else does. His confidence is astounding, but it is not foolhardy. David doesn't offer himself for the challenge as a martyr; he takes the challenge believing in his heart that he can win it. Instead of focusing on the strength and experience of his opponent, David chooses to focus on his own attributes and draws on his previous successes to give him hope. He recalls how God has given him strength in the past to fight off the lions and bears that attacked his sheep, declaring, 'The Lord who rescued me from the paw of the lion and from the paw of the bear will rescue me from the hand of this Philistine' (v. 37).

Saul is reluctant to send David into the fight, but, because no one else has come forward, he has no choice. As David isn't a warrior, he has no armour, so the king calls for his own armour and makes David put it on. David isn't used to wearing armour, and it feels heavy and cumbersome—so much so that he can't even walk while wearing it. To the onlooker, just when it looks as if David's fate can't get any worse, it does. Even Goliath is insulted to see this fresh-faced youth walking towards him, carrying a shepherd's staff. He says, 'Am I a dog, that you come at me with sticks?' (v. 43). But David knows he is not a warrior, and he doesn't plan to fight Goliath as a warrior. To him, Goliath is just another wild animal to be felled. Staying true to his own strength, David doesn't try to be anything or anyone he is not. He simply picks up some stones and fires a shot from his sling, just as he has probably done hundreds of times before while out in the fields. The stone hits Goliath smack on the forehead and, with that one blow, the giant who has so terrified everyone falls to the ground, dead.

There is a school of thought which argues that David's victory was not as improbable as we once thought. Perhaps Goliath was so large because he had a medical condition called acromegaly, in which the body produces too much growth hormone. Acromegaly can cause visual impairments, which could account for Goliath's reference to 'sticks', when David was carrying just a single staff. Even if it is true that Goliath was not as strong as he was perceived to be, these new perspectives only serve to make it even more inspiring as a story of hope. Hope isn't about holding out for the impossible; it is about believing that what God has placed on our hearts is possible, even when other people want to tell us otherwise.

Hebrews 6:19 describes hope as a sure and steadfast anchor of the soul. It is an image I like because it gives me a picture of hope as something that keeps me grounded and stops me drifting off into the waters of fear and despair.

Hope is my connection to God. Hope keeps me thankful for all the blessings he has given to me in my life. It stretches my concept of what's possible and gives me the courage to face challenges that may seem impossible. Even though the circumstances may look, from the outside, to be pointing one way, I don't know the whole story; only God does.

TODAY'S PRACTICE

1 Find 15 minutes in your day to sit quietly, close your eyes, take in a couple of deep breaths to help you relax, and be still in the presence of God. Imagine you are breathing in God's love and breathing out anything that is troubling you.

2 We all have our own 'giants' in life—obstacles that seem impossible to overcome. The question is, are we going to be like David and concentrate on what we know to be true about ourselves and all the reasons why we could succeed? Or, like the rest of the Israelites, are we going to focus on the size and strength of our giants and all the reasons why we are bound to be defeated? Think about something that God has helped you overcome in the past, which you thought was impossible. Approach today's challenges with confidence and the positive expectation that what God has placed on your heart, he will help you to achieve. You can't see the full picture—only God knows that—so don't assume that everything is against you. Instead, remember with thanks the good that God has done for you in the past and use it to strengthen your hope that, in God's strength, you will find a way through again.

3 At the end of the day, spend five minutes thinking about any good things that have happened and things that you have enjoyed. Fill the space for today's diary entry. Don't stop

writing until the space is full. It doesn't matter how big or small the thing is that you choose to write down. All that matters is that you are noting something good that happened today. When you have written your list, thank God for all the things that are on it.

DAY 40

YOU MADE IT!

He who began a good work in you will carry it on to completion until the day of Christ Jesus.

PHILIPPIANS 1:6

We have reached the end of our 40-day journey together, but in many ways, for you, this is where the real journey begins. The Bible uses '40 days' as a spiritually significant time in which God prepares people for his work. I hope that in these last 40 days you have gained a clearer idea of how God is speaking to you in your life and feel more confident that you have a significant role to play in the ongoing creation of the world.

Mother Teresa once said, 'I never look at the masses as my responsibility. I look at the individual.' Changing the world for the better starts with you, and the way you interact with every person you meet. Of course, there will be times when you don't act as you might like, when you feel tired, stressed and vulnerable. Don't let this put you off from following God's wider vision for your life. God is always waiting for you, where you are. Just pick yourself back up and, through his grace, start again.

Change is a gradual process. If you were to do the exercises in this book in a few years, or even a few months, your experience would be different. I hope that you have benefited from the exercises and that there are some you might consider incorporating into your life. Today, however,

I would like you to celebrate. Give yourself a treat; look back over your diary for the past six weeks and remember how far you've come and all the good that God has worked in your life. Pray that you will recognise every circumstance as an opportunity to love, and that your eyes will continue to be opened to the wonder, beauty, joy, creativity and miracles of each day.

NOTES

1 *Burden of disease from environmental noise: Quantification of healthy life years lost in Europe*, WHO, 2011: www.euro. who.int/en/health-topics/environment-and-health/noise/ publications/2011/burden-of-disease-from-environmental-noise.-quantification-of-healthy-life-years-lost-in-europe.

2 *A focus on the nation's viewing habits from TV Licensing*, TeleScope, 2011: www.tvlicensing.co.uk/ss/Satellite?blobcol=urldata& blobheadername1=content-type&blobheadervalue1=applic ation%2Fpdf&blobkey=id&blobtable=MungoBlobs&blobw here=1370006220747&ssbinary=true.

3 The Revd Arthur J Dobb, *A History of the Diocese of Manchester: Like a mighty tortoise*, Upjohn & Bottomley, 1978.

4 Amanda J. Rose, et al., 'An observational study of co-rumination in adolescent friendships', *Developmental Psychology*, Vol 50(9), Sep 2014, pp. 2199–2209: http://psycnet. apa.org/index.cfm?fa=buy.optionToBuy&id=2014-30815-001.

5 Danny Dorling, *Inequality and the 1%*, Verso Books, 2014.

6 M. Maltz, *Psycho-cybernetics*, Prentice-Hall, 1960.

7 P. Lally, et al., 'How are habits formed: Modelling habit formation in the real world', *European Journal of Social Psychology*, Vol. 40, pp. 998–1009, Wiley, 2010.

8 Humphrey Primatt, 'A Dissertation on the Duty of Mercy and Sin of Cruelty to Brute Animals', T. Cadell, 1776.

9 Carmel Thomason, *Every Moment Counts: A life of Mary Butterwick*, DLT, 2011.

10 www.366daysofkindness.com.

11 General information on kindness research can be found on The Random Acts of Kindness Foundation's website www. randomactsofkindness.org.

12 'Volunteering and health: what impact does it really have?' (Institute of Volunteering Research, 2008): www.ivr.org.uk/ ivr-news/133-volunteering-and-health-what-impact-does-it-really-have.

13 www.gallup.com/services/169328/q12-employee-engagement.aspx.

14 A. Wrzesniewski, C.R. McCauley, P. Rozin and B. Schwartz, (1997). 'Jobs, careers, and callings: People's relations to their work', *Journal of Research in Personality*, Vol. 31 (1997), pp. 21–33.

15 David Lykken and Auke Tellegen, 'Happiness is a stochastic phenomenon', *Psychological Science*, Vol. 7, 3 (May 1996). pp. 186–189; Alexander Weiss, Timothy C. Bates and Michelle Luciano, 'Happiness is a personal(ity) thing: The genetics of personality and well-being in a representative sample' *Psychological Science*, Vol. 19, 3 (March 2008), pp. 205–210.

16 Fulton Oursler, *Modern Parables* (Doubleday Company Inc., 1950).

Against the Odds

True stories of healing and forgiveness

Carmel Thomason

Forgiveness is central to our faith because it is central to life. No relationship can survive without the ability to forgive, but sometimes we are hurt so deeply or so often that forgiveness appears impossible.

This collection of inspirational true stories demonstrates the healing power of forgiveness through ordinary people's experiences of war, crime, terrorism, betrayal, relationship breakdown and the uncertainty of life's path. Aimed at both individual reflection and group study, each story is followed by thoughts from a practitioner or church leader, which can be used to open a conversation about what you've just read, and questions to help you think about the wider issues raised.

Wherever you are in your life right now, this uplifting and practical book will encourage you to think about your own experience of forgiveness—how you might make this gift an everyday part of your life, let go of pain, restore relationships and live your life to the full.

ISBN 978 1 84101 739 6   £8.99
Available from your local Christian bookshop or direct from BRF: please visit www.brfonline.org.uk.

Walking with Gospel Women

Interactive Bible meditations

Fiona Stratta

Imaginative meditation can be a powerful way of attuning ourselves to God's presence, involving as it does the emotions as well as the mind. This book offers a refreshing and inspiring way into Bible study, using meditative monologues based around many of the women of the gospels. Through a time of guided reflection, we identify with the woman concerned and see what lessons emerge for today as we ponder her story.

Each chapter consists of a monologue, linked Bible passage and discussion material designed to draw out deep communication and group fellowship, as well as transformational learning. While designed primarily for small groups meeting to grow their relationships with God and with each other, the monologues can also be used as a way into silent reflection either for individuals or with larger groups (for example, the monologues could be adapted to use in Sunday worship—for intercession, a time of reflection or as part of a sermon).

ISBN 978 0 85746 010 3   £7.99
Available from your local Christian bookshop or direct from BRF: please visit www.brfonline.org.uk.

Walking with Old Testament Women

Imaginative studies for Bible meditations

Fiona Stratta

The world of the Old Testament can seem remote, yet if we take a meditative approach to reading its stories, we can find ourselves connecting the people and events of those far-off centuries with our own lives. *Walking with Old Testament Women* follows the same imaginative, Ignatian-style approach as Fiona Stratta's well-received first book, *Walking with Gospel Women*.

Taking twelve women characters, some familiar, some less-known, Fiona uses monologues and reflective questions to explore what their experiences can teach us today. Suitable for both group and individual use, the book offers a gentle introduction for those who have not encountered the stories before, but can also be a refreshing resource for those who feel they know the stories well.

ISBN 978 1 84101 718 1   £7.99
Available from your local Christian bookshop or direct from BRF: please visit www.brfonline.org.uk.

Rhythms of Grace

Finding intimacy with God in a busy life

Tony Horsfall

Rhythms of Grace emerges from a personal exploration of contemplative spirituality. Coming from an evangelical and charismatic background, Tony Horsfall felt an increasing desire to know God more deeply. At the same time, he felt an increasing dissatisfaction with his own spiritual life, as well as concern at the number of highly qualified and gifted people involved in Christian ministry who experience burn-out.

In this book he shows how contemplative spirituality, with its emphasis on realising our identity as God's beloved children and on being rather than doing, has vital lessons for us about discovering intimacy with God. It also provides essential insights about building a ministry that is both enjoyable and sustainable.

Includes questions for reflection and action at the end of each chapter.

ISBN 978 1 84101 842 3   £7.99
Available from your local Christian bookshop or direct from BRF: please visit www.brfonline.org.uk.

The Recovery of Hope

**Bible reflections for sensing God's presence
and hearing God's call**

Naomi Starkey

We live in the hope of experiencing first-hand the all-sufficient grace, love and forgiveness which is God's alone, a hope that we may know with our heads long before we feel it in our hearts. This book is centred on a hope that means encountering God not only as consoling presence in the darkness but as one who challenges us to respond to his call. That call may prove to be costly, but as we respond, we will find ourselves transformed as we discover and rediscover not only that we are known exactly as we are, but loved beyond understanding as God's precious children.

In a series of Bible reflections—and some poems—the theme of this hope is explored in different ways, from the yearning of the Psalmist to walking the gentle journey of the Good Shepherd's leading.

ISBN 978 0 85746 417 0   £8.99
*Available from your local Christian bookshop or direct from BRF:
please visit www.brfonline.org.uk.*